Buoyancy:

Building Resilient Kids

Dr. Kirk Austin

Buoyancy: Building Resilient Kids

Cover by Vooys Design (www.vooys.ca)

ISBN: 9798647232229

In acknowledgement of some of the people I care about that demonstrate buoyancy on a daily basis.

- Dawna - your resilience, tenacity, and excellence in the face of Multiple Sclerosis is exceptional.
- Mervin - your endurance and hope in the face of Parkinson's disease is inspirational.
- Gregory - your bravery and acceptance in the face of cancer is extraordinary.

Contents

Buoyancy: What is it?

Breathing is like an anchor in the midst of an emotional storm: the anchor won't make the storm go away, but it will hold you steady until the storm passes.

~Russ Harris~

In the history of professional sports, few athletes enjoy "name-recognition," where everyone knows who you are. Even fewer athletes have names that exemplify their game. In golf, names like Tiger Woods, Jack Nicklas or Annika Sörenstam come to mind. In football, names like Tom Brady or Joe Namath represent the best of their era. In men's and women's hockey, Gretzky and Crosby or Campbell and Wickenheiser were the best their time. Pick any sport, and there are athletes who have climbed to the top of their profession and held its attention as the *best-of-the-best*. And so, it is with basketball.

In the past three decades, few teams have dominated the sport of basketball more than the Chicago Bulls and the Los Angeles Lakers. Their dominance at the height of their play is legendary. They were basketball dynasties. They seemed unbeatable.

In the 1990s, the Chicago Bulls won the NBA championship six times in nine years. They were so dominant that they won the championship three years in a row, twice. That's right, two "three-peats." For their part, the Los Angeles Lakers won a total of five NBA championships in the 2000s.

Players like Michael Jordan and Scottie Pippen come to mind when people talk about the Chicago Bulls. Players like Kobe Bryant and Shaquille O'Neal come to mind when people talk about the Los Angeles Lakers. These players were at the top of their skills, the top of their game and the top of their sport - for years. Each player made the other better.

Though many sports fans may know both the teams and the players, not many would know the name of the man who is at the center of all of them. The one name that ties both teams and players together is Phil Jackson. He was the central figure in both the Chicago Bulls and LA Lakers basketball dynasties.

Having been an NBA player for part of his career, he brought his love of the game to coaching as his time as a player came to an end, and his basketball career evolved. Bringing his unique coaching style to the game, Jackson was the head coach for both teams. He coached the Chicago Bulls in the 1990s and moved on the Los Angeles Lakers later in his career.

In total, Phil Jackson has 13 NBA championship rings. Two, he earned as a player. Eleven others he earned coaching both the Bulls and Lakers. He is arguably one of the most successful coaches in any sport, men's or women's, let alone basketball.

What made Phil Jackson so successful as a coach was a unique combination of his basketball IQ (his understanding of the game and ability to strategize), the talented players that were on his teams, his incredible work ethic, and the unorthodox coaching practices that he used to train his teams.

Like most excellent coaches in any sport, their intelligence in their sport is a given. Most know their game inside and out. Practicing set plays, honing player's skills, and strategizing is all part of their success. And like most winning sports franchises, the quality of athletes contributes to their success. Better players have better skills that help create more wins, especially if players synergize their efforts. And for any team wanting to win, their work ethic is important. Practicing hard contributes to playing well.

One of the most under-rated parts of Phil Jackson's coaching style was his unorthodox coaching practices. It was these uncommon practices that arguably made Phil Jackson so successful. Most coaches of the day worked on skill development and game strategy. Phil Jackson did the same. However, he added elements to his coaching leadership style that other coaches had not done at the time.

Imagine playing a basketball scrimmage in the dark, or sitting in a circle, breathing in sync with your fellow players. These activities would seem odd to players looking to merely enhance their skill. But these activities were part of a coaching style that lead both the Bulls and Lakers to the domination of their sport.

Any coach at any level will tell you that adversity is part of the makeup of the game. How players learn to overcome adversity is important. Skill development and game strategy can help to minimize the effects of adversity. If your team is down by a few points, no problem - "just remember what we practiced, and we can get back in this thing", most coaches would remind their players. But what about when things get *really tough*? At this point, most coaches would hope that their players would call on deeper attitudes and abilities like resilience, courage and tenacity to press on. Some of these could be taught or coached. But the true test of the student's learning them could only be applied in real-life adversity.

For his part, Phil Jackson also coached his players to overcome adversity through skill development and game strategy. But he also taught them something extra. He taught them to *breathe*. That's right - he taught them to breathe.

In particular, he taught them skills related to Mindfulness, a practice of awareness, breathing and surrender. These skills would sound simple, or even odd to a professional athlete. But they were profound when applied. They helped the Bulls and the Lakers achieve unparalleled success.

Any competitor in any sport will tell you that nerves are part of the game. You can play through them, or they can derail your success. Teach players to be aware of their thoughts, emotions, sensations and they have something to address. Teach an athlete to manage their thoughts, and you can help them to quiet the negative ones and enhance the ones that improve their play. Teach them to calm their breathing and they can remain relaxed shooting a three-point shot or at the free-throw line. Managing their breath can calm them in the dying seconds of a high-pressure game. In this way, you can help the players manage the nerves and play better.

Teach someone to 'be in the moment' rather than focusing on winning or losing, and stress will decrease. This surrender will help calm the nerves of each player, maximizing their abilities. Teach them to breathe, and the quality and nature of their breath will influence their game performance and the outcome of the game itself. Some attitudes, skills, and abilities will break your game. And some attitudes, skills, and abilities will build it.

This book looks at 7 characteristics deeply connected to life success. They promote human strength and flourishing. They are characteristics that contribute to personal achievement and to *human buoyancy*. And they can all be built, practiced and developed.

I have always liked the idea of buoyancy. It is the quality related to rising-up or staying above the waterline. Rather than sinking, the buoy on the ocean remains above the waterline due to the air that it holds within it. Most are made of heavy hardened metal, but still, they remain afloat. Even when storms rage and surge around them, they stay above the waterline.

In the same way, the book will look at the stories of seven people. Each story tells of how the person remained buoyant rather than sinking under the weight of their incredible trials. Each person remained irrepressible, unsinkable, and continued on, rising to the tests that each one faced.

The stories are arranged using the acronym BREATHE. Each letter represents an element of human buoyancy. They help people to remain 'up' during life's challenges. They are Bravery, Resilience, Endurance, Acceptance, Tenacity, Hope, and Excellence.

- **Bravery** considers the attitude and actions related to *pressing on* despite trials, fear, challenges, or adversity. The real-life mountaineering drama of friends and climbers Joe Simpson and Simon Yates is discussed.

- **Resilience** considers the attitude and actions related to *bouncing back* from trials, adversity, challenges, and setbacks. The real-life story of Irish gymnast Kieran Behan is discussed.

- **Endurance** considers the attitude and actions related to *holding on* despite trials, challenges, or difficult circumstances. The real-life story of polar explorer Ernest Shackleton and his men is discussed.

- **Acceptance** considers the attitude and actions related to *making peace* with trials, adversity, challenges, or difficult circumstances. The real-life story of two-sport Paralympian Alana Nichols is discussed.

- **Tenacity** considers the attitude and actions related to *sticking with it*, despite trials, challenges, adversity, or difficult circumstances. The real-life story of marathon and triathlon athletes Dick and Rick Hoyt are discussed.

- **Hope** considers the attitude and actions related to *expecting the best* despite trials, adversity, challenges, or difficult circumstances. The real-life story of cancer activist Terry Fox is discussed.

- **Excellence** considers the attitude and actions related to *doing your best* despite trials, adversity, challenges, or difficult circumstances. The real-life story of dancer, author, speaker, and artist Simona Atzori is discussed.

How To Use The Book

The book is meant to help people build personal Buoyancy. Adults (parents, teachers, and adult helpers) can read it for themselves to promote their own growth and development. If they have children that they support, adults can read it to the children they care for.

Chapters one through eight frame and discuss the nature of Buoyancy. Each element of the BREATHE acronym has its own chapter and tells a story of a person who exemplifies the concept being discussed. Each can be read to children by a parent, teacher or adult helper.

At the end of each chapter, questions are provided to stimulate deeper thinking about the BREATHE concept being discussed. These can be completed by the person reading the book. They can also be used as discussion questions with kids to help them learn about Bravery,

Resilience, Endurance, Acceptance, Tenacity, Hope and Excellence.

Chapters nine through twelve frame how to develop and enhance the skills related to building buoyancy. Exercises are provided to assist with personal learning. Adults can do them for their own growth. Adult helpers, teachers and parents can also help kids learn these skills through assisting them with forms, questionnaires and exercises.

Bravery: Pressing On

The best way out is always through

~Robert Frost~

The day was perfect for their adventure. The sky was sunny, bright, and brilliant blue, and the weather was comfortable and moderate for mountaineering. It was in June 1985. The two men readied their climbing gear, said farewell to their friend, Richard Hawking, who would remain at their basecamp, and began their ascent. They knew that their climb would be challenging, but they were sure that they would reach the summit of the mountain by the end of the day, something that no one had ever done. What was unknown to either man was that by the end of their adventure, both their friendship and their bravery would be tested beyond their wildest imagination.

Joe Simpson and Simon Yates were good friends. They had built their friendship through a mutual love of mountain climbing. Joe was a 25-year-old climber who had unwavering confidence in his mountaineering ability. Simon was the younger of the two men at 21. He was already an accomplished mountain climber and had honed his climbing ability for years. The two had been planning their adventure for some time, and now their goal was within reach.

The aim of their adventure was to climb to the top of a mountain called the Siula Grande. This mountain stood tall at 20,853 feet of elevation. Located in the Andes mountain range in Peru, no one had ever climbed to the summit. It was their hope that they would be the first to reach the top of the mountain - and live to tell about it.

The pair had been climbing for several days to get to the location of their final ascent. They had brought only essential food and gear to minimize the amount of weight that they would need to carry. On the afternoon of the third day, the climbing conditions were perfect for their ascent. The two men began their climb to the top of the mountain.

It was later that afternoon that Joe Simpson and Simon Yates reached the summit of the Siula Grande. They were ecstatic. The two were tired from the climb, but adrenaline elevated their spirits. They were the first people *ever* to reach the top of the mountain! All the time, work, and energy invested in planning the climb had culminated in the joy they felt as they surveyed the fantastic view that the summit provided. They were the first men *ever* to see it.

Despite their excitement, their celebration was short-lived. Both men realized that climbing to the summit also meant that they had to climb back down, and this posed a problem. The men had climbed up in good weather conditions, but the weather had changed since reaching the summit. Large clouds had rolled in, and it had begun to snow. On top of that, the wind made the snow blow about with such force that the men faced white-out conditions. After climbing down for some distance but no longer able to see, they had to stop for the night.

The next morning, the men once again began their descent. What made the climb difficult was that the men were roped together and had to climb down, linked as a pair. The thinking behind this was that since they were tethered if one man slipped, the other would be able to catch him.

Another danger that the men faced was the unforgiving nature of the snow and ice that they walked on. Ice could break away and cause one of them to slip and fall. Snow could also hide deep crevasses that the men could fall through. They had to be careful with each step. They had to go slow.

It was during their descent that something startling happened. Joe Simpson had hoped to drive his ice-ax into the icy mountain as a way of lowering himself. But as he lifted his ax, his feet slipped from underneath him. He fell some 20 feet down the mountain.

20 feet may not seem like a significant distance, but when he stopped, his right leg slammed into the mountain's surface and broke. Both of his lower leg bones broke through where his knee joint was. His pain was incredibly excruciating, and Joe Simpson could no longer stand on his right leg. This made the prospect of climbing down the rest of the way almost impossible.

Both men realized that they were in a dire situation. There would be no steep-angle rescue team coming to save them. There would be no high-altitude helicopter to fly them to safety. Joe Simpson and Simon Yates realized that if they were going to survive, they would have to get down the mountain by themselves. Instead of panicking, they devised a plan.

Their plan required bravery and a daring effort; Simon Yates would lower Joe Simpson down the mountain, little by little. Staying above, Yates would anchor himself onto the mountain and lower Simpson, who had tied their ropes around himself. After lowering Simpson to a suitable area, Yates would then lower himself to his friend. The men would repeat the process again and again until they were off the mountain. If all went according to plan, they could both survive.

At first, their scheme for survival seemed to be going well. Yates slowly lowered his friend in an inch-by-inch descent down the mountain. What complicated the process was Simpson's leg. His pain was extreme. With each lowering effort, his leg would jar and bounce against the snow, and he would scream out in agony. On top of this, the weather was extremely cold, and they had run out of supplies. They had to get off the mountain, or both would die. They pressed on, Yates continuing the process, intent on getting his friend to safety.

Simon Yates successfully lowered his friend several times, but then something unexpected happened. As Joe Simpson was being lowered, he began sliding on a section of ice, and he couldn't stop. As he gained momentum, Simpson slid over a cliff and remained hanging 80 feet above a chasm. Because of the biting cold, his hands were numb, and he couldn't pull himself back up the rope. He yelled up the mountain to tell Yates his predicament, but the howling wind prevented Yates from hearing. Simpson was helpless.

What was worse was that Simon Yates also began to slide. The weight of holding Simpson caused Yate's feet to slip. Knowing that both might die if they fell over the cliff, Yates had to make a terrible choice. He reached for his knife and cut the rope.

Simon Yates was overcome by the weight of his choice. Shock, guilt, and grief pressed in as he was sure that he had just killed his friend. If he had not cut the rope, they would both be dead. In his mind, there was no other choice. With the biting cold and the howling wind, he didn't have time to sit with his flurry of emotions. He had to get off the mountain, or he might die from the elements. Reluctantly, he pressed on and continued his descent down the Siula Grande.

For his part, Joe Simpson remembered dangling on the end of a rope, tethered to his friend, unable to move. The next thing he knew, he was peering upward toward the light suspended above a deep crevasse. He had been helpless. Both men were experienced climbers, and

Simpson knew that Yates had very few choices for survival. He understood his friend's choice to cut the rope.

It seemed surreal to the injured Simpson, looking upward from the bottom of a crevasse. The walls of his glacial prison were enormous, slick, and unclimbable. His leg tortured him with a constant throb of excruciating pain. And as he looked up, he was met with the realization that he had survived an 80-foot drop into the icy cavern but had no means of escape. The walls of the chasm were sheer ice. He didn't have the tools to climb, nor could he lift himself with his broken leg. As he surveyed his options, he realized that he had few options. He could remain still and let himself freeze to death. Or he could look for a way out. This option meant that he would have to go deeper into the icy crevasse.

Any climber will tell you that crevasses are scary, dangerous, and life-threatening. Without a means of escape, a person faces certain death. To descend further into one appears fool-hardy, but this was Simpson's only option. He *was* afraid, but he realized he needed to summon all his bravery to press through his fear. He began pulling himself along the icy floor. With each push deeper into the crevasse, incredible pain shot through his broken leg. Yet he courageously pressed on into the frigid darkness, clinging to the tiniest piece of hope that he might find an escape.

At one point of his expedition deeper into the chasm, Joe Simpson thought his eyes were playing tricks on him. From where he lay, it appeared that the ice looked thinner in a spot just ahead of him. He crawled toward it. To his surprise, a light seemed to be coming from a source just beyond the layer of ice. Summoning all of his available strength, he hammered at it. His fist broke through the ice and revealed the source of light; daylight! By following the floor of the crevasse sideways, Simpson had found a way out of the icy tomb onto the remaining slope of the mountain. He was free.

Very quickly, Simpson realized that despite his freedom from the crevasse, he could not rejoice for long as Simon Yates would likely have thought that he had died in the fall. If Yates thought he had died, Simpson concluded, no one would come looking for him. Once again, he had to summon his courage to press on.

It had taken days for him and Yates to climb to the summit of Siula Grande. He reasoned that if Yates considered him dead, he might leave their original basecamp shortly after he got there. Simpson knew that he had to pull himself the rest of the way to their camp if he was to have any hope of getting off the mountain alive. And this would take time and an incredible effort.

The journey was long, cold, and painful. To move, Joe Simpson had to push his body with his good leg while pulling himself with his upper body, which was already nearing exhaustion. He was unable to walk, and attempting to hop would do no good as the broken leg would flop about causing intolerable pain. As it was, the push/pull method of moving himself still caused unbearable pain. Yet he pressed on. He knew he didn't have much time. If he lagged behind, he would be left on the mountain. This would mean certain death.

Between himself and basecamp lay a glacial field punctuated with crevasses. With careful manoeuvring, Simpson reasoned, he could find a way around the crevasses he could see. It was the crevasses that were covered by a thin layer of snow or ice that posed the greatest threat. He knew that if he fell through one of these, there would be no miraculous recovery.

Inch by inch, he pushed himself. Every rock and uneven bit of terrain would cause his broken leg to feel stabbing pain. His body was weak and tired. He was without food and water, and he had become dehydrated. On top of this, he was cold and hypothermic and risked exposure from the elements. Yet he could not rest, as any delay would mean certain death.

Simpson bravely persisted, dragging his broken body across the glacier. As night fell, the bitter cold set in. Exhaustion had taken its toll. Joe Simpson surrendered his effort and stopped pushing his body. In one last effort to be found, he used his remaining strength and called into the night for help.

After cutting the rope, a devastated Simon Yates had made his way back to basecamp. He related the story of losing his friend to Richard Hawking, Yates' and Simpson's mutual friend, who had remained at basecamp while they attempted to summit the Siula Grande. He was heartbroken with the news that Joe Simpson had fallen to his death. Yates had arrived exhausted and spent from his ordeal. The men decided to rest that night and leave the following day. Hawking and Yates climbed into their respective sleeping bags for the night. They would leave basecamp and start the journey down the mountain the next day.

Neither Yates nor Hawking could sleep. Thoughts of their lost friend ran through their minds, and they could feel the cold night's air against their exposed skin. Just beyond the thin fabric of the tent, they could hear the howling of the icy wind. But there was something else in the air.

"Is that a voice?", they both thought to themselves, before dismissing it as an overactive imagination.

But then, they heard it again. It did sound like a voice. But whose? To both Hawking and Yates, the voice calling in the night air was surreal and ghost-like. It sounded like their friend Joe Simpson, but in their minds, he had died and remained in a crevasse somewhere on the Siula Grande.

Again, they heard a voice calling from the night's darkness. This time, both Hawking and Yates jumped to their feet. They ventured into the dark to explore the noise. To their unbelief, they saw a man lying on the ground close to the basecamp. It *was* their friend Joe Simpson! They could not believe their eyes, but there was no mistaking him. Somehow, miraculously, he had made it back to the camp before they left the following morning.

The following day Richard Hawking and Simon Yates were able to coordinate getting Joe Simpson off the mountain to the safety of medical help. It would take some time for the men to rest, heal, and eventually tell their story to the world. Their tale would eventually be told in a book called Touching The Void, written in 1988. A screenplay of the same title was also made into a movie in 2003.

Theirs is a story of incredible bravery in the face of severe and unimaginable adversity. It will no doubt remain in mountain climbing history as a tale of extreme bravery, friendship, survival, and human determination.

Bravery and Buoyancy

Bravery is the attitude and actions necessary to face trials, fear, adversity, or difficulty. Other words for bravery are:

- Courage
- Nerve
- Daring
- Boldness
- Having guts
- Fortitude

Bravery isn't required when you don't face fear or have the perfect skills to accomplish a task. That would be called confidence or ability. Bravery *is required* when fear stands in the way of you performing a necessary task.

Bravery in an essential and necessary element of Buoyancy. Life can be hard at times. It will always present challenges. These challenges can feel deflating.

When trials or difficulty tell you that it's too hard, you're going to fail, or that you don't have what it takes, bravery tells you that you can do it. It encourages you that you're strong enough and that you do have what it takes to face the challenge.

Bravery requires that you at least try, and give your best effort. It requires that you press on and continue moving forward. Fear will challenge you to stop or run away because of the danger that is in front of you. Bravery beckons you onward.

<u>Questions to consider</u>

- What did Joe Simpson and Simon Yates do that was brave?

- What was the biggest danger or difficulty that each man had to face?

- What emotions do you think each man felt during their adventure?

- What would each man have to tell himself to remain brave?

- When have you ever had to be brave?

- What was the trial, danger or difficulty you had to face?

- How did you face your fear?

- How did you encourage yourself to face this danger or difficulty?

- What is one thing you could do that could build your bravery?

Resilience: Bouncing Back

Resilience means you experience, you feel, you fail, you hurt.

You fall. But you keep going.

~Yasmin Mogahed~

To say that he was 'active' was an understatement. Kieran had always been a high-energy kid. But *his* type of 'active' required an intense focus and direction. At the age of 8, he was enrolled in a local gymnastics club. His parents knew that this was the type of activity that could channel his energy into active and coordinated movement. Kieran immediately fell in love with the sport. He was coordinated and strong and was able quickly to understand and follow the instruction offered by his coaches. He was a natural at it and began to excel.

He had been training at his local club for a few years and had grown strong and agile through discipline, practice, and hard work. But Kieran noticed that something wasn't quite right in one of his legs. It was the dull pain that didn't seem to go away. His doctor ran medical tests and found the source of the problem. He had a tumour. The good news was that it was benign and was not cancerous. The bad news was that he would have to undergo surgery to remove it.

Kieran wasn't scared of the surgery. But he didn't like the idea of taking time away from his gymnastics training. It was during the operation that the unexpected happened. Kieran experienced complications during the surgical procedure. These complications left him unable to use his leg. For the next 15 months, Kieran Behan would have to navigate his world using a wheelchair.

Using a wheelchair can be fun for a lot of kids - racing up and down hallways, popping 'wheelies' and such. But for a high energy kid, it can also be very restricting. By the end of his 15-month rehabilitation, Kieran was ready to begin his gymnastics training once again. He started with simple movement and activity. These were to measure whether he could put full weight on his leg. Building his strength, agility, and capacity meant that he needed to press through any discomfort or pain.

Gradually, Kieran was able to increase the type of activity that he could perform and the weight that it required. He was resilient and determined to bounce back from his injury. Before long, he was performing the same activities that he had trained for in the year before. Little did he know that he would need his resilience once again before he would compete at the highest level of gymnastics.

He had trained hard and had completely bounced back from his injury. His coaches were amazed at how far he had come in such a short time. But one morning, while training on the high bars, Kieran had a severe accident.

In gymnastics, high bars are an apparatus that holds a polished metal bar that spans horizontally (sideways). The gymnast uses the bar to showcase their strength and agility as they usually spin their body around it. Most high bars stand approximately 3 meters or 9 feet high off the ground. In an unfortunate turn of events, young Kieran Behan hit his head and landed on the ground while doing a routine. It was a serious accident, so severe that it left him with a significant brain injury.

Kieran's brain injury left him with considerable balance and coordination problems. He couldn't stand on his own. Instead, he was once again limited to a wheelchair. Cartwheels, tumbles, and high bars were out of the question. He was now forced to learn how to sit up without falling over.

Part of Kieran's injury impacted his inner ear. This meant that balance was significantly impaired. Turning his head too quickly, or at an odd angle could make his balance fail, and he would fall over. He was even forced to relearn how to turn his head. His doctors informed him that he would most likely never be able to train in gymnastics again. They were doubtful that he would have the balance to even walk again.

The doctor's news would have been crushing for most gymnasts. But Kieran knew that he had something that many athletes didn't have - a 'never give up' type of attitude. He was determined. And he was resilient. He wasn't going to give up just yet. Instead, he set little goals and worked hard at regaining his ability.

At first, he worked on his balance. When he could turn his head without falling over, he began to work on sitting up on his own. Little by little, Kieran began to regain his ability. With hard work, he recovered his capacity and strength. It would take three years, but Kieran Behan defied all expectations and began training in gymnastics once again, winning awards as a junior gymnast in his home of Ireland.

Kieran continued to train, work hard, and improve. He had gained strength, stamina, and agility, and it showed in his routines. Eventually, Kieran was invited to compete internationally. In 2010 while performing in a competitive routine, he felt a sharp pain in his knee. "Oh no", he thought. "What now?"

The doctors were quickly at his side to assist. To his dismay, they reported that he had seriously injured his knee. Kieran had torn his anterior cruciate ligament (ACL). This would mean more time to heal and rehab his knee. He was just six short weeks away from competing in the European championships.

Kieran would once again work hard at his rehabilitation, exercising his resilience. He worked hard at regaining his strength, stamina, and agility. After a short time, he was once again ready to compete. But once again, he would rupture the ACL, this time on his other leg, leaving him to work at healing all over again.

Many athletes would reflect on their involvement in their sport during this time. Perhaps it would be time to give it up, quit, or retire. Kieran Behan was not one of those athletes. Instead, he assessed the damage that his body had experienced and decided to recover, work hard, and begin training in gymnastics when he was ready.

Once again, Kieran decided to work hard at rehabilitation and training. Once again, he regained his strength, stamina, and agility, working diligently on his routines. Eventually, he was ready to compete. In 2011 Kieran competed and won a bronze and silver medal at the World Challenge Cup and European Championships.

His trials, recoveries, and success had drawn the attention of the gymnastics community. He was *good*. And he had bounced back from so much adversity already at such a young age. But rising in talent meant that he was invited to competitions in other countries. This meant incurring costs for flights, food, and hotels. He had overcome the physical challenge. Now he faced a financial challenge.

Exercising his resilience once again, he began thinking about how to raise money to do the sport he loved. With the help of friends, family, and his home community, he raised money through bottle drives and bake sales. Soon, he was able to travel to international competitions.

Kieran participated in Olympic qualifying events in 2012. His hope was to compete in the 2012 Summer Olympics held in London, England. He performed well and finished in fourth place, just out of the medal standings. Because of his strong finish, he was able to compete in London. He performed his routine well but did not win any medals that day.

Ever resilient, once again, he trained hard, adding to his strength, agility, and performance. Four years later, he once again qualified for the 2016 Summer Olympics in Brazil. Once again, he performed his routine to the best of his ability. But once again, his performance fell just short of the gold, silver and bronze medallists.

During his gymnastic career, Kieran Behan had demonstrated incredible resilience. He had refused to let an injury keep him from the sport he loved. When surgery slowed his training, Kieran bounced back through effort and hard work. When a brain injury compromised his balance and confined him to a wheelchair, he worked hard at his rehabilitation and bounced back. When his ACL's were torn on both knees, he kept going forward. Despite not winning a medal, one of his greatest acts of resilience came at the 2016 Rio Olympics in Brazil.

At the beginning of his routine, Kieran Behan felt a 'pop' in his knee. He had dislocated it. Dislocation meant that his knee didn't work as it should. It meant significant pain and discomfort. Despite the pain and possibility of falling, Kieran continued to roll, tumble and perform. He pressed through and did what he had to do. He completed his routine to a roaring crowd.

Kieran wouldn't win a medal this day. He was fortunate to just complete his routine, given the state of his knee. But he had once again demonstrated exceptional resilience - just as he had, every other time of his career when he had faced trials and adversity.

Resilience and Buoyancy

Resilience is the attitude and actions related to *bouncing back* from trials, adversity, and challenges. Other words for resilience are:

- Adaptable
- Flexible
- Bounce back
- Durable
- Irrepressible

Resilience is not required if you never experience difficulty or setbacks. It *is* required when you are knocked down or blocked from your goal.

Resilience is a necessary and essential part of Buoyancy. Life circumstances will sometimes knock you down. Adversity may tempt you to give up, to believe it's too hard to try again or to remain stuck. Resilience encourages you to try again, to persist, and to take one more step. It calls you to bounce back and try again.

Resilience means that you might get knocked down with the experience of adversity. But it calls you to get up again, and to face the challenge head-on. Resilience calls you to bounce back and continue toward your goal.

<u>Questions to consider</u>

- What did Kieran Behan do that was resilient?

- Of all of his injuries, what was the biggest adversity that he had to face?

- What emotions do you think he felt during his trials?

- What would he have told himself to remain resilient?

- When have you ever had to recover from adversity?

- What was the trial, adversity or challenge?

- How did you feel during this challenge?

- How did you face your feelings?

- How did you encourage yourself to face this danger or difficulty?

- What is one thing you could do that could build your resilience?

Endurance: Holding On

Endurance is patience concentrated.

~Thomas Carlyle~

His ship was christened the 'Endurance' after his family's motto - 'By endurance we conquer'. It was extremely modern for its day - a three-masted, wooden schooner, equipped with the most advanced gear for a polar expedition. One feature of the boat was its coal-burning steam engine that would guarantee power, force, and forward momentum. This would ensure that it would make headway in icy conditions. And with the 28 seasoned sea-faring men that he recruited, Earnest Shackleton was sure that he would accomplish his mission. The year was 1914.

Shackleton's mission was impressive. He would make his way to the Antarctic through the Weddell Sea, south of South America. When they landed, he and his men would traverse the polar icecap by dog sled team. His dogs were the best of the best. They were reliable and agile, able to pull the heaviest load. And Shackleton was a seasoned Captain, used to guiding sailors and used to lengthy expeditions. Despite knowing this journey would be tough, he remained confident about their success. Little did he know at the outset, that this journey would become one of the greatest stories of survival in nautical history.

Beginning in late 1914, the Endurance and its men set sail toward the South Pole. Given the time of year, thick chunky ice slowed their progress, and by mid-January, the ship had come to a complete stop. It had become frozen in its place. Shackleton had his men took turns trying to free the boat, but it was no use. The Endurance was held fast by polar ice. It would remain stuck and unmoving for the next 11 months. The weather was cold and unforgiving. But the crew endured the subarctic temperatures and biting winds trying to remain optimistic.

The men kept busy day after day by doing chores and playing games. But in late October of 1915, the ice began to shift and compress. The ice, as it froze, began to expand, and given the conditions of the sea, it began to move. It squeezed the ship from all sides. The Endurance began to break apart, its wooden structure was no match against the power of the crushing ice. Shackleton knew that it was a matter of time before the Endurance sank to the bottom of the sea. He abandoned his ship after removing what provisions could be recovered. On November 21, 1915, the Endurance slipped beneath the ice and was gone.

Three small wooden rescue boats were among the materials retrieved from the Endurance before she sank. These boats were essential to their very survival. To the world around them, they were lost at sea and presumed dead. They had not made it to their destination and could not send word back for help. Ever the optimist, Shackleton called their ice flow 'Patience Camp', making the best of his circumstances. They would call this home for five more months.

When it is very cold, the sea freezes into huge sheets. But in certain conditions, ice also breaks apart into smaller pieces. The ice on which "Patience Camp" rested was becoming more likely to break apart, separating the crew and supplies. Knowing that their time was limited, Shackleton planned a daring escape.

He loaded the three small boats with men and supplies and set sail toward a tiny island that was 100 miles away. They would need to sail into the open ocean for five days just to get to land. Elephant Island, as it was called, was a piece of frozen rock in the middle of nowhere. It was home only to the ocean animals. It sustained no other life. When they arrived, it was the first time the men had stood on solid ground in almost 500 days.

Shackleton knew that despite getting to Elephant Island, they would die if they stayed. No one was coming to rescue them. He also realized that with the food and drink that remained, and the sea animals that they could catch, they couldn't stay indefinitely. Shackleton devised a long-shot plan for survival.

The plan had terrible odds, but it was their only hope. They would need to sail 800 miles on the open ocean in a small wooden boat to reach the island of South Georgia. This island had a whaling station, and enough supplies and resources to save every-last-man. Shakleton chose his best crew members, boarded a small lifeboat, and set sail.

These were seasoned and gifted sailors. They were used to sailing great distances and horrible conditions. But this was different. They only had a sextant as a navigation tool. This was a rudimentary instrument that they would point at the stars in order to calculate direction.

However, given the terrible weather and violent seas and cloudy night skies, this was incredibly difficult. If they made a mistake in their calculations, it would mean missing their destination by hundreds of miles. Everyone would die. Shackleton had to be exact. There was no room for miscalculation.

Once in the open water, they experienced rough seas. This was not the lively surf of a warm-weather vacation. These were violent and freezing seas. The water itself would freeze to their small boat, weighing it down. With the added weight, the boat could sink. Cresting waves would also splash into their boat, threatening to drown all aboard. Taking turns, each man would climb onto the boat and chip away at the ice.

The waves were enormous, and any misstep could mean certain death. The men had to endlessly bail seawater from the boat. Taking sextant readings required that one man would need to stand on top of the boat to gain sight of the stars, at the height of enormous sea-swells. Two other men held his legs to offer balance and support. The whole time, the boat would be staggering from the turbulent waves. All aboard were soaked with frigid water.

The men were freezing, wet, and frostbitten by the subarctic temperature and severe winds. Sleep was sporadic and broken. Yet after 14 days on the relentless seas, they arrived at the island of South Georgia, exhausted from their journey.

Shackleton realized that they had a problem. They had arrived safely at the right island. But they had arrived on the wrong side of the island. Their boat had been so badly beaten by the seas it was no longer safe to sail to the other side. Again, Shackleton devised a daring plan - they would cross the island on foot. Between their position and the whaling station on the other side were mountains and glaciers with deep crevasses. Having only the resources that they had sailed with, they began their journey.

The men took screws from their boat and mounted them through the soles of their boots, making a crude type of crampon. This would offer traction on the ice. Enduring the wind, cold, and the snow, they climbed the mountains. They were exhausted, freezing, and hungry.

Yet they navigated the mountains, glaciers, and hidden crevasses.

With each step, the men pressed onward toward their goal. They climbed for thirty-six hours straight, after sailing for 14 days on merciless seas. They eventually arrived at the whaling station on the island of South Georgia to the utter disbelief of the townsfolk.

It would take several months to rescue the men left behind on Elephant Island. But in late August 1916, Shackleton arrived back at Elephant Island and rescued the remainder of his crew. No one had died on their adventure. They had endured two years of captivity in one of the most hostile places on earth. It was truly a miracle.

Endurance and Buoyancy

Endurance is the attitude and action to withstand danger, difficulty, or adversity. It is necessary when the journey towards a goal is met with resistance. Other words for endurance are:

- Stamina
- Grip
- Staying power
- Holding out
- Hanging on

Endurance is a vital and essential part of building Buoyancy. Challenges in life can sometimes go on for quite some time. These difficulties can feel demoralizing and deflating. Endurance pushes you to hold on during these times.

Adversity will challenge you to give up, or try to convince you that you can't take much more. Endurance will encourage you to keep going and to persevere. Endurance will tell you that you're not done just yet. Endurance means that you continue to hold on to your goals or dreams regardless of the challenge.

Questions to consider

- How did Earnest Shakleton show endurance?

- What was the biggest difficulty that they faced?

- What emotions do you think they felt during their adventure?

- What would they tell themselves to endure?

- When have you ever had to endure something?

- How did you feel during this challenge?

- How did you face your feelings?

- How did you encourage yourself to face this difficulty?

- How could you build your endurance?

Acceptance: Making Peace

I can be changed by what happens to me. But I refuse to be reduced by it.

~Maya Angelou~

Understanding is the first step to acceptance, and only with acceptance can there be recovery.

~J.K. Rowling~

Alana Nichols remembered how hard it was to learn. Snowboarding was not easy at first. The standing up part of snowboarding was natural. But any movement down the hill meant that she could lose her balance, catch her heal- edge or toe-edge, sprawling and falling onto the snow in a not-too-graceful heap.

Catching her toe-edge would throw her body forward. She could land on her knees, elbows, or hands. This would hurt, but she could push herself up to try again. To catch her heal edge meant that she would be whipped violently backward, landing on her tailbone or the back of her head. This would really hurt and leave her with headaches. She had lived through all the falls and bruises and survived. Neither one was fun. She would simply tell herself that this was all part of learning.

Alana had gotten better at snowboarding since her early beginnings. She was far better, in fact. She had learned the art of turning with either her toe or heal edges with equal ease. She had mastered the gracefulness of using the board against the slope and curve of the mountain. She especially loved deep powder with its billowy turns, or holding her body in a compact position and going fast downhill. Her balance was excellent through years of snowboarding in the mountains in Colorado. She could almost always recover mid-fall and land herself with the agility of a cat, perfectly landing on her feet. She exuded confidence in her ability and always wanted to learn, pressing into the next trick to master its complexity.

This is where her memory was a bit fuzzy. She remembers people standing over her asking if she was OK. She remembers trying a trick, a backflip, off a jump. And she remembers her mid-air thought that she was over-rotating and would not 'stick' the landing. What she couldn't understand is why she couldn't move.

The paramedics were assessing, "Ms. Nichols, where does it hurt?" At first, she didn't respond, her head was spinning, trying to make sense of it all. Again, they pressed, "Alana, can you move?" She would later come to realize that she had rotated too far while doing her flip and had landed on her back on a rock. She had broken her back and was now paralysed from the waist down. She was 17 years old.

After some time, she had gotten used to the routine. The doctor's visits, the hospital food, the rehabilitation. She had even gotten used to the wheelchair. Never one for self-pity or giving up, she accepted her new reality and pushed her body's ability to learn. And now, with her new means of transportation, she was able to deftly handle acceleration, corners, and even a few tricks on four wheels. Within two years of her accident, she was able to navigate her daily routines with ease. In fact, her athletic drive and curiosity eventually led her to explore a new activity - basketball.

It has been said that "anything worth doing is worth doing poorly, at first". Like anything we learn, it is hard at the beginning, then it gets easier. Alana had to learn to accelerate or stop her wheelchair while handling a basketball. She then had to learn to do it with other players buzzing around her. And she had to learn the game itself, the rules, the strategy, the passing, the scoring - all of it. But Alana Nichols was a quick study of the sport, and within no time at all, she was proficient at it.

She would play with other wheelchair athletes, watched what they did, picked up the nature of the sport, and learned from them. It was even quite fun. Before long, the University of Arizona contacted her. They had seen her ability on the court. And they were impressed with her basketball ability. They offered her a scholarship to study at their school while playing for their wheelchair basketball team. She studied education while she attended.

Alana Nichols continued to study at the University of Arizona and play wheelchair basketball. Within two years, she was selected to play in the 2004 Summer Paralympics on the U.S. Women's team as an alternate. The following year she was selected for the United States national women's team. She continued to practice, play, learn the game, and get better.

Within a few short years of her accident, she was excelling in her brand-new sport. She didn't look longingly backward at the loss of her ability to walk, run, or snowboard. Instead, she had accepted it and found a way to move forward. She practiced hard, and she played hard. In 2006, she played on the women's team that won the silver medal at the Wheelchair Basketball World Championship. Alana continued to apply herself, and big things were still ahead.

Alana's basketball talent was exceptional. Her work ethic, basketball ability, and her commitment to her team and teammates eventually got her noticed once again by the selection committee for the women's national wheelchair basketball team. She and her teammates would represent the U.S.A. and compete in the 2008 Paralympics in Beijing.

During the Paralympics, they played well against all the other teams. They continued to win. In the final game, Alana Nichols and the U.S women's team won the gold medal. Germany would win the Silver medal, and Australia would win Bronze. This accomplishment overshadowed that during this time, she had continued to attend school. She had continued to work on and complete her Master of Arts degree in kinesiology, another major success that Alana set out to achieve.

Since her snowboarding accident, Alana had focused on her education as well as her basketball career. It had all gone so well. But in the back of her mind, she wondered if she would ever get back to the mountain slopes of Colorado. She missed the snow. Nothing really compared to the feel of cold, crisp mountain air, or the feel of carving a perfect line in untracked snow; or of speeding down a steep incline of a mountain ski run - the body holding the perfect tension between control and chaos. It wouldn't take long before Alana Nichols would rediscover her passion for downhill.

The month following the Beijing Paralympics, Alana returned to Colorado and began training in the sport of adaptive alpine skiing. She was naturally athletic, and her ability to learn the sport was exceptional. Her form of adaptive skiing allowed her to remain in a sitting position in a modified style of chair. The chair itself was positioned atop a ski mounted directly under her.

It took a lot of practice to balance and remain upright at first. But once she got the hang of it, it was no problem. To help with balance, she held on to adaptive ski poles - one in each hand. These looked like regular poles but had a small singular ski attached to the end that contacted the snow. As she skied down the slope of a mountain-run, she would lean her body to the left or right to steer. As her body and ski turned, she would set the ski poles down like outriggers to help with balance and turning. It took no time before she was skiing more challenging terrain with ease.

Alana had watched the Winter Paralympics in 2006. She was impressed with how talented the pool of skiers was who competed in the alpine events. They went so fast and turned so adeptly as they shot down the mountain at blinding speed. She wondered if she could ever be able to compete at the level of the other Paralympians. Learning of the National Sports Centre for the Disabled (NSCD), she began to explore what it might take to advance in her new sport to be able to compete at a high level.

Alana began training in the alpine skiing program at the NSCD and was an immediate success. She learned the art of using her body and balance to pick more aggressive lines down the mountain. She improved her speed and shaved valuable seconds off her times. Before long, she was participating in actual races with other competitors.

To say that she was competitive was an understatement. Alana worked hard at her sport to get better and better. She didn't just want to race or go fast -

she wanted to WIN. In 2009, Alana Nichols won her first race. It was a Super-G event at the North American Cup, where she placed first ahead of other competitors.

Slalom races are ones that require skiers to race down a mountain course while navigating their way around poles (gates) anchored in the snow. The fastest one down, successfully navigating the gates, without falling, wins the race. Super-G's are different. The name is short for "Super Giant Slalom." This race requires that skiers race down a large twisting section of the mountain, going as fast as they can to the finish line. The fastest one down without crashing wins the race. But this is the trick - NO CRASHING.

Because skiers are trying to shave seconds off their recorded time, they go very fast. If it were a straight line, '*not crashing*' would be easy. The Super-G, however, has twists and turns. Too fast, and a person can lose an edge on their ski, slip, and fall wildly onto the snow spinning out of control. Alana skied fast, and in control for the whole race. In a few short years, she had returned to the mountains and won her first race, edging out other highly skilled competitors.

Alana Nichols would continue to perform well in the sport of adaptive skiing. She had won her first Super-G and went on to finish in third place in the super-combined race the same year. She would go on to win or place second or third in the alpine downhill, Super-combined, or Super-G races the following year. And later in 2010, she decided to compete in the Winter Paralympics held in Whistler, British Columbia.

Once again, Alana competed in multiple events. And once again, she brought her competitive spirit and skied well against fierce competition. At the end of the games, Alana Nichols had won or placed in several events. She came home decorated with two gold medals, one silver medal, and one bronze medal. In doing so, she became the first woman *ever* to win medals in both summer and winter Paralympics.

If she had asked, "Why me?" or remained stuck in self-pity after she failed her attempt at a snowboarding backflip, she would never discover the sports of wheelchair basketball or adaptive skiing. And the world would never know of her accomplishments in both sports. Instead, she met her circumstances with acceptance. Then, surveying her options, she picked herself up, dusted herself off, and moved on to the next adventure with passion, drive and determination, and a solid desire to excel.

In doing so, Alana Nichols excelled in wheelchair basketball and adaptive downhill alpine skiing to a level not seen by many athletes. She remains an inspiration to both disabled and able-body athletes around the world.

Acceptance and Buoyancy

Acceptance is the attitude and action to tolerate or make peace with trials, difficulty, challenges, or adversity. Acceptance is not wishful thinking for a different outcome. It is not a passive endurance of a difficult circumstance. Other words for acceptance are:

- Embrace
- Integrate
- Welcome
- Becoming OK with
- Making peace with
- Affirming

Acceptance is an indispensable part of building Buoyancy in your life. There are times in life where things happen beyond your control. The difficulty will tell you that you face the worst possible thing and that you can't take much more of it. Acceptance will encourage you that it's OK and that you *can* make peace with it.

Acceptance is an active tolerance or making peace with your situation. It is learning to let-it-be while continuing to press towards a goal.

Questions to consider

- What did Alana Nichols do that showed acceptance?

- What was the biggest adversity that she had to face?

- What emotions do you think she felt during her rehabilitation?

- What would she have told herself to remain accepting?

- When have you ever had to demonstrate acceptance?

- What was the adversity?

- How did you feel during this challenge?

- How did you face your feelings?

- How did you encourage yourself to face this danger or difficulty?

- What is one thing you could do that could build your acceptance?

Tenacity: Sticking With It

We can do anything we want to if we stick to it long enough.

~Helen Keller~

If I asked you to think of famous sports duos, you would most likely think of basketball greats like Lebron James and Dwyane Wade, or tennis greats like Serena and Venus Williams. You might even think of hockey stars like Sydney Crosby and Evgeni Malkin, or Wayne Gretzky and Mark Messier. Regardless of WHEN they played their game, they remained elite athletes with incredible work ethics. On top of that, each player made the other one better. One would not have been the same without the other.

Now, if I asked to think of father and son duos that played the same sport, you would most likely think of race car drivers Mario and Michael Andretti, or football greats Archi, Peyton, and Eli Manning. The list could go on. However, if I asked you to name famous father and son duos that competed in the same sports at the same time, you might struggle to name even a few, especially if they competed in more than one sport. One father-son duo participated in marathons, triathlons, and other endurance sports for *three decades* and yet they remain mostly unknown to the general public. And like other "greats", each made the other one better.

In 2014, Rick and Dick Hoyt completed their last Boston Marathon. This is a type of foot race that covers great distances and requires incredible tenacity. The Boston Marathon covers a distance of 26.2 miles or approximately 42.2 Kilometres. The first Boston Marathon was held in the year 1896. It has been run every consecutive year since, for over a hundred years. Its worldwide popularity drew runners from all over the world- each would have to qualify for acceptance into the race, just to run it.

What made this race special for the father and son duo was not *just* that they qualified for it and were running in it, but that it was the *32nd time* that they were running in it. What was more exceptional was that Dick, the father, was already in his mid-70's and Rick, the son, was in his 50's.

Rick's love of running began in his childhood when he asked his dad if he could run in a charity event that would help raise money for a fellow student who had recently become paralysed. He had never run before, so the idea was new to his parents. In fact, Rick had never even taken a step on his own before. What's more, he had only recently learned to communicate through the help of a computer.

You see, Rick was disabled and couldn't walk or talk. He needed the help of others to move about and required the use of a computer to put his thoughts into words to communicate. His father loved the idea of running to help the other student and agreed to help Rick run in the event. This was the beginning of Team Hoyt.

Like all great athletes, there are times when they are young that a person is not quite sure if beginning a sport is a good idea, or if they have the tenacity to keep going. In his case, Rick was born with cerebral palsy. This means that his umbilical cord was somehow wrapped around his tiny neck before he was born. This limited the blood flow to his developing brain and body. The unfortunate result was that his brain would send signals to nerves and muscles that would not respond in the correct manner. Some early doctors believed that Rick would not amount to much and told his parents that he would be better cared for in a permanent care-facility for disabled people. Other doctors told the Hoyt's to treat Rick like any other child. That's exactly what they did.

In his early years, Rick's mother would talk to him and try to stimulate his learning. She knew he was smart. He would follow her around with his eyes and watch her do everything around the house. When he was old enough, she would teach him the alphabet, the sounds of words, and the names of things. Before long, Rick was understanding and learning.

Still unable to communicate verbally, his parents eventually found him a computer that allowed him to translate his ideas into sentences. He was now able to communicate! They soon realized that Rick was quite smart. He was enrolled in school and participated in classes with other students. Rick went on to complete high school and eventually completed a university degree in Special Education. During his career he worked in the computer department of Boston College.

When Rick first asked his father to help him run in the charity event, the Hoyts weren't sure how it would go. They first had to find a way to make it happen. One problem that they faced was that Dick was not a runner and was already getting close to 40 years of age. He had to train to build enough stamina for the race.

They also had to configure a mobility vehicle to make running with Rick easier. Dick would have to push Rick the whole way. This would require endurance-training and tenacity. They had no idea at the time that their first run together would spark a decades-long love of competing together. Nor did they know that both Rick and Dick Hoyt would become famous for their endurance races. But by the end of their first race, they were hooked.

When they talked after their first race, Dick was obviously tired. He hadn't been training as a runner for long. But Rick exclaimed, "Dad, when I'm running, it feels like *I'm not handicapped*!". This was all that Dick needed to hear. If his son wanted to run, he was going to help him to run.

To get in better running-shape, Dick would wait until Rick was at school, then he would load bags of cement mix into a modified wheelchair/stroller that Rick would eventually sit in for races. The point behind this was for Dick to build strength, endurance, and sheer tenacity to run in more races. To his son's delight, they were able to do more than the initial charity race. Before long, they added a second race, then a third.

Over time, the duo added more and more races to their agenda. In fact, they began to race in longer distance races, eventually adding marathons to their schedule. They would race whenever they could. At one point, the duo even began to add triathlons to their racing schedule. This meant that both would need to run, swim, and bike a great distance. Of course, since Rick could not actively coordinate the use of his arms and legs, these race activities would be complicated. However, with some planning, designing better equipment and endurance training, they were able to complete even in triathlons.

Triathlons are long-distance races that require running, biking, and swimming. Both Dick and Rick had enough running-races under their belt that they felt confident in this part of any triathlon. However, they needed to figure out how to bike and swim together.

For the biking component, Rick would sit at the front of a modified bike in a chair that could hold his body. During races, Dick would peddle and steer the distance required for the race. Rick would cheer his dad onward. For the swimming component of the race, Rick would sit in a small boat, and Dick would provide the muscle power and navigation to complete the course. Again, Rick would provide encouragement.

The first triathlon was hard. But then they added a second, then a third. By the end of their three-decade-long sports career, Dick and Rick Hoyt had completed a total of 72 marathons and 6 Ironman triathlons (each one, a 2.4-mile swim, a 112-mile bike ride, and a 26.2-mile run).

So prolific was their career that by the time they retired, the Hoyts had competed in 1,130 endurance events. They even crossed the United States in 45 days during the summer of 1992 by both running and cycling as a means of raising awareness of the possibilities for persons with a disability.

They had originally called themselves Team Hoyt when they began racing in 1977. And their message was clear to all people who wondered if they too could compete, regardless of disability - "Yes You Can!" The example of their sheer tenacity has inspired millions of people who have heard about their races.

Both Dick and Rick provided a three-decade-long example of what love, commitment, and tenacity can do.

They eventually developed a non-profit organization called the Hoyt Foundation to inspire and advocate for individuals with disabilities in the United States. Though they stopped competing in endurance sports, both Dick and Rick have remained active in their Foundation and through speaking at community events.

In 2013, nearing the end of their long-distance running, swimming and biking career, Dick and Rick Hoyt were honored by the City of Boston, near the site of the Boston Marathon. They had competed in the race for 32 years. In their honor, a life-sized brass statue of the two of them was dedicated to Team Hoyt, recognizing their tenacity and lifetime achievements in long-distance racing and disability advocacy. The motto that Dick and Rick lived by was forever memorialized on the statue - "YES YOU CAN!"

Tenacity and Buoyancy

Tenacity is the attitude and action to persist or be determined regardless of obstacle or challenge. It is *sticking with it*, despite trials, challenges, adversity or difficult circumstances It requires a dedicated focus toward a goal. Other words for tenacity are:

- Grit
- Doggedness
- Determination
- Will power
- Stick-to-it-iveness

Tenacity is a necessary and important element of Buoyancy. Some challenges in life make you feel like you are losing your grip. Difficulty will try to convince you that you are too tired, that you can't keep going, or that it's taking too long. Tenacity will encourage you to take one more step, to do just a bit more, or to press on a little farther.

Tenacity involves a continued and unrelenting effort in the same direction. It requires that you stick with your determined effort toward a desired outcome.

<u>Questions to consider</u>

- What did Rick and Dick Hoyt do that showed tenacity?

- What was the biggest adversity that they had to face?

- What emotions do you think they felt during their races?

- What would they have told themselves to remain tenacious?

- When have you ever had to be tenacious?

- What was the challenge?

- How did you feel during this challenge?

- How did you face your feelings?

- How did you encourage yourself to face this adversity?

- What is one thing that could build your tenacity?

Hope: Expecting The Best

Hope is a waking dream.

~Aristotle~

The discomfort that he felt in his side was more of a dull, aching sort of pain. It wasn't going away like any other cramp or pulled muscle would. Instead, it was lingering. Resting didn't seem to be helping this time. He knew that this would mean stopping for a bit, just to get checked out.

He had just run a marathon or at least the equivalent to one, so it felt. Actually, he had run a virtual marathon each day for the past 143 days. He had come such a long way, and he had so much more to do. Little did he know, Terry Fox wouldn't run again after this day, but his actions would stir millions of people around the world with his vision of hope.

He wasn't big for a kid, but he was gritty and determined. Like most Canadian kids, he played street hockey and other sports too, like baseball, basketball, and even running. Though he was never the best athlete based on raw talent, the one thing he was known for was his grit and determination. He would work hard and use his dogged determination to continue well into any sport. It was this mental toughness that would serve him as he got older and played in his preferred competitive sports.

Terry awoke one morning with pain in his right leg. He couldn't stand on it, and it wouldn't bear his weight. "I must have done something in practice," he thought to himself. Terry always practiced hard and played hard. He had been playing basketball for a university team, and perhaps he had just hurt it without knowing. But after a few days and some medical examination, his prognosis was clear.

As it turned out, Terry had not tweaked his knee or pulled a muscle. Instead, he had been diagnosed with a cancerous tumor. His doctors assured him that with the advances in medicine that he would at least have a 50/50 chance of survival. There was one catch - they would have to remove his leg.

One of Terry's old basketball coaches came to see him before his surgery. The doctors had informed him that they were going to remove his leg six inched above his knee. It was going to be major surgery. His recovery was going to take a long time. The coach, wanting to cheer Terry on, brought a magazine for him to read when he recuperated.

One story that caught Terry's eye was of a runner who had completed a marathon. What caught his attention was that the runner was an amputee and had run the marathon with one natural leg. As Terry thought about his future, he began to dream about what he would be able to do without one leg. What if he could do the same? Before long, he was planning to run across Canada.

Rehabilitation was hard. Learning to walk on crutches was the easy part by comparison. But learning to walk on an artificial leg meant learning to deal with the pain associated with connecting it to the stump of his amputated leg. Then there was also the issue of balance. That was hard enough, but later to try to walk added another steep learning curve. Terry had already learned to be determined and focused. It was what made him a fierce competitor. When he set his mind to something, he did it. For Terry Fox, learning to walk was not enough. He wanted to run.

For all his competitiveness and determination, one could easily overlook that Terry Fox was also kind and compassionate. While learning how to navigate his world without a leg, he spent time rehabilitating alongside other sick kids. What gripped him was the pain that many of them had to endure or the prospect that they didn't have much hope for their futures. "What if," he thought, "there was a way that we could find a cure for cancer." The compelling hope for a cure for cancer would drive his vision to run across Canada.

Learning to walk on his prosthetic leg was hard. He would take a step with his left foot and have to raise his hip on its right side and wait for the plastic leg to spring forward. He had to focus on balance at the same time, trying to make it all look and feel natural.

Running on his prosthetic leg was a steep learning curve. To run meant that as he propelled himself forward with speed and momentum, he had to hop on his left leg after landing in stride, to give his right leg enough time to spring back into stride. This stutter-step running method was difficult to master but eventually became more rhythmic.

Terry's vision of running across Canada was taking shape in his mind. He would run to raise awareness of cancer and also to raise money in the hope of finding a cure. It was his Marathon of Hope. But he would need to build his endurance for longer distances. Terry trained for 15 months, running every day. His stump had healed well enough, but the prosthetic leg would rub back and forth with each stride, often leaving it raw and bruised. As he trained, he was able to add more and more distance as the days passed. Before long, he was running 23 miles every day.

As his dream began to take shape, he was able to convince a friend to drive a van alongside him and make the meals. He also needed visibility and endorsement. He wrote a letter to the Canadian Cancer Society stating his intent to run across the country. His vision was to earn money that would benefit cancer research. After some convincing, they agreed to support his dream.

In April of 1980, Terry Fox dipped his artificial leg into the Atlantic Ocean of Eastern Canada and began his run. On some days, the weather was sunny and enjoyable to run in while other days would offer sweltering heat. These days felt oppressive to run in. Some days the weather would offer cold rain, or sleet, or blast him with gusts of strong winds. Each day, Terry would summon the resolve, and run almost 23 miles - regardless of the elements.

Slowly, word began to spread of a young man who had an ambitious dream. Media would cover his daily routine of a one-legged marathon in the hope of finding a cure for cancer. His vision was initially to raise an amount equivalent to one dollar for every person in Canada. At the time, it would equal approximately 24 million dollars. Greater media exposure meant that ordinary people would hear of his Marathon of Hope and contribute financially to his dream. He had run for several months, and contributions were finally starting to accumulate.

By the time he had reached Thunder Bay in Ontario, he was almost halfway across Canada. But he had developed a cough, and he had pain in his chest that was lingering. A medical assessment would reveal that his cancer had returned. This time it had spread to his lungs. Terry Fox would have to stop his Marathon of Hope to undergo treatment. Ever a believer in the dream of finding a cure for cancer, he would continue to advocate for donations for research and for hope until he died on June 28, 1981. He was just 22 years old.

Terry Fox exemplified the attitude and posture of hope. Hope doesn't look backward and dwell on the '*what ifs*' of the past. Hope doesn't remain stuck in the present, focusing on the negatives. Hope leans toward a future that is positive and optimistic. It calls us forward to a future that is constructive and encouraging.

His original dream was to create awareness and a compassionate response to those impacted by cancer. He sought to raise money to continue to research cancer's cure. This hope continues today.

At the time of his death, Terry Fox had raised just over 24 million dollars, his original goal. But his Marathon of Hope was just beginning. Building on his legacy, soon after his death, other cities in Canada would host a Terry Fox Run (760 locations participated in the first year). Before long, other countries began to host Terry Fox Runs to raise money for cancer research in the hope of finding a cure.

Since his death, each year, people from all over the world participate in races that honor Terry's original vision of hope. To date, over 750 million dollars have been raised worldwide in support of this vision and message of hope.

Hope and Buoyancy

Hope is the attitude and action of optimistic expectation. It is *expecting the best* despite trials, adversity, challenges or difficult circumstances.

Hope is not based on imagination, or fantasy, or unrealistic aspiration. It is a positive and compelling vision of a possible outcome. Other words for hope are:

- Optimistic
- Heartful
- Encouraged
- Positive outlook
- Full of promise

Hope is a crucial and essential ingredient in building Buoyancy in your life. Some challenges in life are hard. They can make you feel deflated, demoralized, or defeated. Hope can make you feel optimistic a buoyed during these times.

Difficulty will try to convince you that there is no use to keep trying. It will nag you that "*Tomorrow will be more of the same*". It will suggest that "*There's no point*" in your effort.

Hope whispers that tomorrow will get better. Hope encourages us that there is a positive conclusion just over the horizon. Hope nudges us that we *have to* keep going.

Hope is the captivating vision that compels the attitude and actions required to make the outcome possible. Hope is expecting the best.

<u>Questions to consider</u>

- What did Terry Fox do that demonstrated hope?

- What was the biggest adversity that he had to face?

- What emotions do you think he felt during his rehabilitation or cross-Canada run?

- How do you think he felt having to stop running?

- What would he have told himself to remain hopeful?

- When have you ever had to demonstrate hope?

- What was the trial, challenge or adversity?

- How did you feel during this challenge?

- How did you face your feelings?

- How did you encourage yourself to face this adversity?

- What is one thing you could do that could build your hopefulness?

Excellence: Doing Your Best

Do more for the world than it does for you.

~Henry Ford~

Excellence is the gradual result of always trying to do better.

~Pat Riley~

She hadn't thought much about what she wanted to be when she grew up. Such thinking was well beyond the scope of any 4-year-old. All she knew was that she loved to create. At the moment, young Simona Atzori loved to paint. When she looked at a blank canvas, the world opened up to her. She could imagine shape and form and color and texture. Before she knew it, she was painting.

Despite her young age, she was quite good. She had never taken lessons or gone to school for art. For that matter, she didn't even know how to read yet. She was the age of an average preschooler. To this point, she was mostly self-taught. But what made her work stand out was that she did it, all of it, by using her feet.

Simona was born in 1974 without any arms. Her first few years were like any other baby - mostly being cared for by her mother and other adult helpers. However, they noticed that there was something special about her. She was energetic, smart, creative, and full of life. Like many small children, she learned to explore her environment through her senses. Where most children reach for things using their hands, Simona would reach with her feet.

Through repetitive use, she became quite adept at reaching, grasping, and holding things. Her feet and toes worked as well as most children's hands and fingers. It was early on that she began to hold pencils and paintbrushes and express her creativity on paper through line and color. Her mother and other adult helpers tried to fit her with prosthetic arms, but young Simona would always resist. To her, artificial arms were too clumsy, bulky, and restrictive. She preferred the ease of using her feet and toes.

Her work was eventually noticed by Italian artist Mario Barzon. He had learned to paint by holding brushes in his mouth. He had been disabled earlier in his life and had become recognized for his art. As he saw her art, he instantly recognized the talent that young Simona possessed. He introduced her to the world of mouth and foot painting. At the age of nine, she received a scholarship from the Association of Mouth and Foot Painting Artists of the World (AMFPA). This organization worked as a non-profit society that helped disabled artists through advocacy, promotion, and sale of their art. Simona's art was now being seen by a wider audience.

Though painting was one of her passions, it was not the only one. She was creative and energetic, and she liked to move her body. By the age of six, she wanted to dance. Her dream was not just to prance about like most impulsive six-year-olds. Simona wanted to move like professional ballerinas, with power and strength and grace.

Her desire to dance was initially met with resistance from teachers who couldn't imagine her as a typical able-bodied dancer. They couldn't see past her disability. Simona was anything but average. She was tenacious and determined and supported by the people who loved her. She was eventually granted her wish and began dance lessons.

As she grew older, the command of her painting had excelled. Her drawings and paintings had become more refined and recognized. She began to paint lifelike images of people, some of them famous. One of her paintings was of Pope John Paul II. The Vatican, having learned of her painting, granted her an audience with him. Simona presented him with the portrait during their meeting.

What's more, the command of her art extended beyond painting to her ability to dance. She was a student of excellence, in art and in movement. She was coordinated, strong, and graceful, and she had an eye for choreography. In 1996 she left Italy and attended the University of Western Ontario in Canada, where she studied Visual Arts. She graduated at the top of her class, refining further her ability in art, form, and movement.

Now recognized for her art globally, Simona's paintings would eventually be exhibited In Austria, Canada, China, Greece, Spain, and in her home country of Italy. Her paintings would inspire others all over the world to look past the limitations of disability to see the beauty of their creations.

Critically recognized for her strong dance ability, Simona was also invited to perform for diverse audiences around the world. One such performance was in 2006, where she danced in the opening ceremony at the Paralympics in Italy. Another such performance was in

2017, where she performed a choreographed dance at the Vatican for Pope Francis.

Simona Atzori continues to inspire others around the world through her creative contributions. Since beginning her quest for excellence, she has won multiple awards for her influence, imagination, creativity, and art. She created her own dance company, SimonArte, in 2010 and continues to dance, choreograph and perform to enthusiastic audiences.

Her paintings are exhibited globally, and in recent years she has begun to write. To date, she has written several books and is a sought-after speaker. Through all of her life and creativity, she has exemplified excellence, encouraging all of us to respect diversity, pursue happiness, and enjoy the exceptional journey that we all experience in life.

Excellence and Buoyancy

Excellence is the attitude and action of being outstanding or extremely good at something. It is *doing your best* despite trials, adversity, challenges or difficult circumstances. It is not a half-hearted attempt at a task, or a mediocre effort toward a desired outcome. Other words for excellence:

- Quality
- Exemplary
- Worthy
- Great
- Superior
- Doing your best

Excellence helps to build our Buoyancy as it always seeks to become *better*. Some challenges will tempt you that you are doing it all wrong, or not good enough, and that you won't get it right. It will tempt you towards apathy or indifference.

Excellence will encourage you that you are off to a good start, that you can do it, and that you are better today than yesterday. It doesn't take mistakes or failure personally. Rather, it tries to *learn* and *grow* from them.

Excellence is not perfection - ever critical and unaccepting of the non-ideal. Excellence simply requires the best effort that you can offer. It involves your desire to learn from your mistakes, to become *progressively better*, bit by bit, and to discipline yourself in the direction of your desired goal. Excellence merely requires that you do your best, every time you do something.

Questions to consider

- What did Simona Atzori do that demonstrated excellence?

- What was the biggest adversity that she had to face?

- What emotions do you think she felt during her painting, dancing or writing?

- What would she have told herself to continue to pursue excellence?

- When have you ever had to pursue excellence?

- What was the trial, challenge or difficulty?

- How did you feel during this challenge?

- How did you face your feelings?

- How did you encourage yourself to face this adversity?

- What is one thing you could do that could build your excellence?

Building Buoyancy

In school, you're taught a lesson then given a test. In life,
you're given a test that teaches you a lesson.

~Tom Bodett~

Have you ever watched a baby learn to walk? It really is a fantastic accomplishment. Just a few short months before trying to walk, every child does very little more than lie wherever they are placed. They eat, they sleep, and they make noises. The only way that they can move around is if an adult helper picks them up and places them in a different spot.

With time, the baby generally becomes aware of their surroundings, still unable to move themselves from where they are located. In curiosity, they turn their little heads, arch their bodies, and reach for things. Before long, they wiggle themselves toward the thing they are interested in. With still more time, they learn to lift their little bodies onto their knees and hands and learn to crawl toward the things that catch their curiosity. And shortly after that, they learn to pull themselves into a standing position while holding on to a stabilizing object like a table or chair.

It doesn't take much longer for a baby to learn to walk after learning to stand. Once standing, they practice walking, all the while holding onto an object to stabilize them. With practice, they learn to find a sense of balance, clumsy rhythm, and muscle control. Then, when they are ready, it happens. Usually, there is a caring parent nearby, coaxing them to walk a few steps toward them. The child tentatively lets go of the object that they are holding onto, seeing if this newfound balance will keep them upright. Then they take a tentative step and usually fall, landing softly on their bottom with a gentle 'thud.'

What is impressive is that they don't quit. Instead, they pick themselves off the ground, holding once again to the object to find their balance. Then they let go and take a step all over again. After several attempts - each time trying, failing, picking themselves up, and trying again - they finally take several steps in a row, to the excitement of all who are cheering them on. And then, once they have a taste for this newfound freedom, they keep on practicing until they can run. From there, the world is theirs for the adventure.

Now imagine that every time a child takes a step and falls, the parent rescues the child from the pain of landing on their bottom and carries them around for the remainder of their childhood. Or if the child, upon falling and landing on their bottom, throws up their hands in protest, saying, "This is way too hard! I refuse to try this again!". Of course, both examples are absurd. The first would prevent the child from learning from the natural test of discovery, perseverance, and mastery. The second would prevent the child from learning through their own failure.

Let's face it. Anything worth doing well requires doing it poorly at first. It requires struggle. Anything you had *ever* learned, whether it be walking, cutting your own food, kicking a soccer ball, or learning advanced trigonometry required failure when you first tried it. From struggle, we experience failure. From failure, we move toward basic understanding and make adjustments and course corrections. And from there, we advance toward learning and mastery.

The test, any test, is designed to reveal what we don't know. It is through our awareness of what we don't know that we are able to get better at what we do know. The parent that protects their child from struggle limits their child's learning. The child who gives up after an experienced struggle impairs their own growth. Growth, development, and learning all require that we *face the test*, struggle with it, make adjustments, and persevere.

Most people who are asked to do something that is outside of their comfort zone have to navigate a complex mixture of emotions, sensations, and thoughts. As its name suggests, a person's comfort zone is the place where they feel comfortable. It is the range of activities, skills, and abilities that a person has already learned. They are *comfortable* using them. There is little risk of failure. Their emotions, for the most part, are calm. Their comfort zone is comfy, cozy, and non-threatening. They are in relative control.

For many, learning buoyancy begins largely outside of one's comfort zone. Bravery often faces danger and requires personal risk. Resilience means picking ourselves up one more time, while the memory of falling down is still fresh in our mind. Endurance means holding on when it is hard. Acceptance means making peace with an uncomfortable option while facing difficulty greater than our own control. Tenacity often faces adversity that requires holding on beyond our natural capacity. Hope means looking for a positive future while you are still in a difficult present. Excellence requires doing our best when others might be slacking and taking the easy route.

The TEST

Whether bravery, resilience, endurance, acceptance, tenacity, hope, or excellence - all require some form of struggle (and overcoming) in the face of complex emotions, sensations, and self-talk. Buoyancy is built like a muscle. Through activation and use, it grows little by little.

Think of building buoyancy as facing a particular test to develop the capacity for bravery, resilience, endurance, acceptance, tenacity, hope, or excellence. The word TEST is useful in understanding the nature of our struggle and how to overcome it.

- The first "T" represents the particular trial that we are facing at a given point in time.
- The "E" represents the emotions that correspond to our perception of the trial and our belief in our ability to deal with it.
- The "S" represents the bodily sensations that occur as we face our trial.

- And the final "T" represents the thoughts that we tell ourselves about the trial and struggle.

Any momentous struggle that we face engages all of these. It is our awareness of them, and response to them that can promote buoyancy's development. Poor responses can limit our growth, healthy responses can build it.

I remember one of the first times I had to do a public speech. It was absolutely terrifying. I wasn't particularly shy or retiring as a kid. I had friends, I was popular, had a sense of humor, and was generally likable. Speaking to my friends was easy. It was well inside my comfort zone. But there was something about having to talk to an audience that felt ominous and foreboding. It was adversity that I had not had to face up until this time in my life. It felt like a capital "C" challenge with big stakes attached to it. It was a test that I thought I would *fail*.

For many people, public speaking may not be difficult. We all know someone who can naturally hold a crowd's attention and communicate with ease. I admire these people. At the time, I knew I was not one of them. The "Trial" that I had to face was the prospect of speaking in front of lots of people. The "Emotion" that I was acutely feeling was fear. As far as the intensity of fear goes, it wasn't quite panic, but it certainly was close to it. When I thought about speaking at the event, even weeks before, I had unusual "Sensations" in my body. I would feel 'butterflies' in my stomach. I would hold tension in my shoulders and get headaches. I would catch myself breathing in a shallow pattern. Sometimes I would catch myself holding my breath. And when I thought about speaking, the "Thoughts" coursing through my mind were all negative and critical. "I am going to blow this.", "I am going to look so stupid.", "I need to get out of this."- all populated my thinking.

The TEST Worksheet example illustrates how I would identify each emotion, sensation, and thoughts based on the trial I faced.

TEST Worksheet Example

Trial	Giving a public speech
Emotions	Anxiety, Close to panic
Sensations	Butterflies in stomach, tense shoulders, headaches
Thoughts	"I am going to blow this.", "I am going to look so stupid.", "I need to get out of this."

As far as unexpected trials go, most of us are unfamiliar with their territory. They are untraveled. They are outside of our control and predictability. And the common emotion connected to most of them is fear. If you think of 'fear' like a swimming pool, there are shallow-end words for fear, like alarmed, concerned, and anxious. The deeper we get into the pool, the words we use to describe our intensifying emotions are more like dread or panic.

It is the "big-ness" of our perception of the trial that influences the intensity of these emotions. And it is the content of emotion that carries with it a sensory component. We feel it in our bodies. Finally, it is essential to know that we all tell ourselves a story about the trial we are about to face. These are our thoughts about how big the trial is, or how prepared we are to face it. Fear-based thoughts convince us that the trial is too big and that we are too small, too ill-equipped, and will likely experience some form of pain or disaster.

What many people don't realize is that during unexpected trials, much of what happens in our minds and bodies occurs without our conscious awareness. We are confronted by a trial and walk around with a knot in the pit of our stomach, or wonder why we have tension headaches. Or we don't reflect with any intensive awareness at the nature and content of our thoughts. During these trials, we are sometimes our own worst critics. Beginning to become aware of our emotions, sensations, and thoughts is an important and necessary beginning of building buoyancy.

Just for fun, recall a time when you had to face a trial that was well beyond your comfort zone.

- What was the trial?
- When you think about it, try to reflect on the time of life that you were in.
  - How old?
  - What grade?
- In reflection on your trial what were the emotions that you remember feeling?
  - Alarmed? Anxious? Dread? Panic?
- In thinking about it, what were some of the sensations that you remember feeling?
  - Where in your body did you feel them?
- What did you think about the size of the trial, or your ability to face it?
  - What thoughts went through your mind?

- o What kind of self-talk did you have?
- o Positive? Negative?

Look at the TEST worksheet on the following page and complete the sections pertaining to the Trial, Emotions, Sensations and Thoughts that you went through at the time. Give it a try. Do your best.

Note: One reason that this exercise has value is that it helps a person become aware of what they are experiencing when they face a trial. Many people are unaware that they experience anxiety or fear, that their breathing is shallow or that their thoughts are critical or catastrophic. Writing out their trial, emotions, sensations and thoughts is helpful, clarifying and insightful. With practice, it gets easier.

TEST Worksheet

Trial	What was the trial? How did it impact you?
Emotions	What were the emotions you faced? Alarmed? Anxious? Dread? Panic?
Sensations	What sensations did you experience? Where in your body did you feel them?
Thoughts	What were the thoughts that you told yourself? Were they positive? Negative?

Chances are that as you think about that time, you can recall that you felt over-matched. The size of the trial appeared more prominent than the resources you believe that you possessed at the time. Most likely, the primary emotion (besides feeling overwhelmed) was in the family of fear (alert, alarmed, concerned, anxious, fearful, dread, or panic). And you most likely felt it somewhere in your body.

Like most people, your thoughts would gravitate to the problem and remain there as you ruminated on how to get past it. And now, if you successfully got past the trial, you probably recognize that you changed as a result of it. You probably grew and learned something about yourself and your ability to overcome.

This is the nature of trials. Some are small, and we can deal with them with little stress. Others are big, and it takes all of our resources to face them. Fear is common during these trials. If we listen to fear and submit to it, we face almost certain defeat. Buoyancy requires that we learn to face our fear, manage it, and find a way through the trial. By learning to manage our breathing, bodies, and thoughts, we can develop the skills to press through almost any trial - big or small.

Breathing

Most of us do it without thinking. We breathe. Every minute of every day, the average person breathes between 12 to 16 times per minute - when they are at rest. That's approximately 20,000 times per day. Obviously, when we exercise, we breathe faster. When at rest, we breathe slower. Not many people realize that there are differences in the nature and quality of the way we breathe. When we are scared, we breathe differently than when we are calm.

If you ever ask a small child to pretend that they are afraid, they will do something instinctive. They will make their face look scared with a furrowed little brow. They will hold their arms in front of themselves with their clenched little fists. And they will pull their shoulders forward, and round their back as if to mimic a turtle. The interesting thing is that their breath will become more shallow. And so it is with fear.

When people are fearful, they breathe differently than when they are calm or confident. When scared, a person will breathe more shallow, more from their upper lung, and as a result more quickly. This action mobilizes a person to face their fear - most often through a fight, flight, or freeze response. When a person is relaxed, their body is more open. As a result, their breath is slower and goes deeper into their lungs.

One trick of building buoyancy is to become aware of the nature of our breath and slow it down. Though facing a trial normally provokes the emotion of fear - buoyancy requires that we breathe in a calm and measured way. For this to become deeply rooted in a person's ability, it takes practice. It takes practice to become aware of our emotions, sensations, and thoughts, and it takes practice to breathe in a way that promotes buoyancy. On the following pages are practice exercises. Give them a try. Do your best.

Practicing Awareness

This exercise is about *"noticing"* your emotions, sensations and thoughts. Begin the exercise by getting into a comfortable position. Take a slow deep breath in. Gently hold it. Then slowly exhale. Repeat, taking a slow deep breath in, then slowly exhale. As you read each item, try to notice what it asks.

1. Do you notice your hair touching your scalp?
2. Do you notice the weight of your ears?
3. Do you feel the bridge of your nose?
4. Do you notice your lips touching your teeth?
5. Do you notice the pressure of your sock?
6. Do you notice your mind drifting?
7. Do you notice your emotion? What is it?
8. Do you notice your shirt touching your skin?
9. Do you notice the coolness of the air on your body?
10. Do you notice the air as it goes through your nose?
11. Do you notice the wrinkles in your hand?
12. Do you notice your thoughts?
13. Do you notice how deep you are breathing?
14. Do you notice the sound of silence?

Note: One reason that this exercise has value is that it helps to bring our attention to what we experience. Most of us can go through our whole day, without becoming aware of what we feel, sense or think. With practice, we get better at noticing.

Body Scan

This exercise is about *"focusing"* your awareness. Begin the exercise by getting into a comfortable position. Take a slow deep breath in. Gently hold it. Then slowly exhale. Repeat, taking a slow deep breath in, then slowly exhale.

1. Draw your attention to your forehead. Notice how it feels.
2. Notice how your eyes feel. Are they relaxed? Tired? Alert?
3. Notice your jaw. Is it tense? Relaxed?
4. How do your lips feel? Do they feel the room temperature?
5. Now draw your attention to your neck and shoulder muscles. Are they tight or relaxed? Can you relax them by thinking?
6. Can you feel the air pass through your nostrils? Is it cool?
7. Notice your stomach rise and fall with each breath. *Remember, breathe slowly in, and out.*
8. Notice the weight of your body as gravity pulls on you?
9. Notice your leg muscles. Are they tight? Tired?
10. How do your knees feel? Any aches or pressure?
11. Notice your ankles and feet. How do they feel?
12. Become aware of your toes. How do they feel?
13. Breathe slowly in. Gently hold. Breathe slowly out.

Note: One reason that this exercise has value is that it helps to focus our attention to what we experience. With practice, we get better at focusing.

Putting It All Together

It's the small pieces that help us understand the bigger picture.

~unknown~

Let's try a quick little experiment. Whatever you do, DON'T think about a flying pink unicorn. Just… don't…think… about… a flying pink unicorn!

So my question is, how did you do? Were you able to *not-think* about a flying pink unicorn, or did one pop into your imagination? If you were successful and didn't think of one - well done. For the rest of you - good try.

It's an interesting thing. Identifying a trial is easy. Sensations usually pop up and announce the arrival of a trial of some kind. The pit in your stomach is normally the first sign that you are facing something that you think is daunting. Noticing the emotions that connect with the sensation is also fairly straight forward for most people. Fear, or some element of it, is normal when facing a trial of some kind.

Even noticing the thoughts that cloud your mind can be straight forward to identify. They are the critical ones that forecast our failure. But trying to tell yourself to "just don't think about it" simply isn't a viable option for most people. The suggestion itself only prompts the awareness of the trial, emotions, sensations, and thoughts, and we end up where we began.

The Practicing Awareness and Body Scan exercises in the previous chapter are designed to help a person to become aware of their emotions, sensations, and thoughts. With practice, a person can learn to "check-in" with themselves to explore the nature of their thoughts and feelings. By "checking in," the person can notice the tension in their body and learn to manage it. Of course, this can also focus a person's attention on the trial they face, rather than reducing it. Building buoyancy requires additional skills.

Now let's think about the flying pink unicorn once again. Trying to pretend it isn't there won't make it go away. Telling ourselves to ignore it won't make it go away. But if I ask you to focus instead on a fluffy blue teddy bear, I am giving you an alternative target to think about.

In the same way, if instead of focusing on the trial, you draw your attention to a different thing, the distraction can reduce the magnitude of the adversity *for a while*. The trial will still be there, and eventually have to be addressed. But for the time you are focusing on the teddy bear, you will have a bit more peace.

The "Grounding" exercises on the following pages help to draw our focus away from the trial by giving us something sensory to focus on. With practice, we get better at doing it and manage our focus for longer periods of time. Give them a try. Do your best.

Grounding: Fingers

This exercise is about *"focusing"* your awareness. Begin the exercise by getting into a comfortable position. Take a slow deep breath in. Gently hold it. Then slowly exhale. Repeat, taking a slow deep breath in, then slowly exhale.

1. Hold the palms of your two hands together.
2. Feel the gentle pressure between them.
3. Now, create a space between your palms and touch just your finger tips together.
4. Gently rub your finger tips together.
5. Feel the gentle sensation between them.
6. Now, focus your attention on just your index fingers.
7. See if you can focus all of your attention on the sensation of your right index finger.
8. See if you can focus all of your attention on the sensation of your right middle finger.
9. Repeat step 8, but rotate through all of your fingers.

Note: One reason that this exercise has value is that it helps to focus our attention to what we experience. Most of us can become highly focused on the trial (adversity, challenge or difficulty) in front of us. This can cause us to get stuck in uncomfortable sensations, emotions or thoughts. Grounding with our fingers allows us to notice, and focus on, the sensations that we feel in our fingertips. This distracts us from our uncomfortable sensations, emotions or thoughts. With practice, we get better at it.

Grounding: Toes

This exercise is about ”*focusing*” your awareness. Begin the exercise by getting into a comfortable position. Take a slow deep breath in. Gently hold it. Then slowly exhale. Repeat, taking a slow deep breath in, then slowly exhale.

1. Turn your attention toward your toes.

2. Try to grab the bottom of your shoe-lining with your toes. Can you do it?

3. Try harder. Concentrate. Can you do it now?

4. If you have carpet, try to grab the carpet with your toes. Can you do it?

5. OK, now you can stop.

Note: One reason that this exercise has value is that it helps to focus our attention to what we experience. Most of us can become highly focused on the trial (adversity, challenge or difficulty) in front of us. This can cause us to get stuck in uncomfortable sensations, emotions or thoughts. Grounding with our toes allows us to notice, and focus on, the sensations that we feel with the tips of our toes. This distracts us from our uncomfortable sensations, emotions or thoughts. It gives our minds something else to focus on. With practice, we get better at it.

Grounding: Breathing

This exercise is about regulating your breathing. Begin the exercise by getting into a comfortable position. Take a slow deep breath in. Gently hold it. Then slowly exhale. Repeat, taking a slow deep breath in, then slowly exhale.

1. As you breath slowly in and slowly out pay attention to your thoughts. Are they busy or relaxed?

2. Try to breathe in for 3 seconds, but exhale for 6 seconds. Can you do it?

3. See if you can do it for 10 breaths in a row. Close your eyes until you are done.

4. Variation: See if you can do step 2 for 5 straight minutes.

5. Variation: Try to imagine each inhale breath coming into your body through your belly button. Imagine the exhale breath leaving through your belly button.

6. Variation: Try to imagine each breath entering and exiting your body through your heart.

Note: One reason that this exercise has value is that it helps to focus our attention on our breath. Most of us can become highly focused on the trial (adversity, challenge or difficulty) in front of us. This can cause us to get stuck in uncomfortable sensations, emotions or thoughts. Slow breathing relaxes our bodies. The slower exhale activates the calming part of our nervous system and calms our physiology. Imagining breathing through our belly button or heart gives our mind something else to think about than our trial. With practice, we get better at it.

Stinkin Thinkin

Remember the flying pink unicorn? Of course, you do. It hasn't gone anywhere. The "grounding" exercises on the previous pages are useful for drawing our attention away from it and give us an alternative target to think about. They also help us to learn to relax in the middle of reasonably complex emotions and sensations. The problem in practical terms is that the trial that we face still remains, even if we distract ourselves and relax from it for a while.

What is common for most people is that an imminent trial right in front of us tends to fill our whole field of vision. The closer it gets, the more looming it becomes. Our emotions can become heightened, our sensations more intense, and our thoughts more active. In particular, when we have to face trials that feel 'too big', we often have thoughts that provoke a negative spiral. We tell ourselves, "It's too big," "I can't do this," "This is too much for me," and other critical thoughts that catastrophize our situation. And we talk ourselves out of any action that might be productive.

Noticing and becoming aware of our emotions, sensations, and thoughts are the first productive step toward buoyancy. Learning to distract ourselves from the difficult ones can help us to stay in manageable moments for more extended periods of time. But managing our thoughts is a crucial skill in building buoyancy. Managing our critical thoughts and holding on to buoyant beliefs can strengthen it. The following exercises can help with this. Try them. Do your best.

Breathing: Shhh

This exercise is about regulating your breathing. Begin the exercise by getting into a comfortable position. Take a slow deep breath in. Gently hold it. Then slowly exhale. Repeat, taking a slow deep breath in, then slowly exhale.

1. Some people have difficulty quieting their thoughts during breathing exercises. So find a pillow or cushion you can use.
2. Hold the pillow or cushion against your chest.
3. Give it a big hug.
4. Continue to breathe slowly in and out. Continue to gently hug the pillow or cushion.
5. As you continue to breathe, try to make the sound "SHHHH" for as long as you exhale.
6. Try it again.
7. Repeat the process, but this time close your eyes for 5 breaths.
8. What did you notice about your thoughts?

Note: One reason that this exercise has value is that it helps to moderate our breathing which has a calming effect. It also helps to manage what goes on in our thoughts. With a person's eyes closed, we minimize any visual distractions. And when we make the "SHH" sound, our ears do what they are supposed to do - they listen.

The sound our ears are hearing is ambient white noise which has no discernable features (like music does: percussion, lyrics, etc.). The sound itself is calming. It is hard for our minds to hold critical comments when it is focusing on the easing and calming ambient white noise.

Breathing: Buoyant Beliefs

This exercise is about regulating your breathing and focusing your thoughts. Begin the exercise by getting into a comfortable position. Take a slow deep breath in. Gently hold it. Then slowly exhale. Repeat, taking a slow deep breath in, then slowly exhale.

1. Some people have difficulty quieting their thoughts. What are your thoughts saying right now?

2. Think of one of your favorite buoyancy words. (Brave, Resilient, Enduring, Accepting, Tenacious, Hopeful, Excellent).

3. As you breathe out, say the words "I am _____" (insert the word that you selected, as you exhale). Repeat this process for 10 breaths.

4. As a variation, Say the words "I am _____" (insert each buoyancy word, one at a time per breath, as you exhale). Repeat this process for 7 breaths (One for each buoyancy word).

5. As a variation, think about words that promote your own buoyant self talk (courageous, capable, strong, smart, etc.). Say the words "I am _____" (insert your chosen word, as you exhale). Repeat this process for 10 breaths.

Note: One reason that this exercise has value is that it helps to replace our mind's critical comments with buoyant beliefs. With practice these buoyant beliefs become easier and more natural to say.

Now let's not pretend that building buoyancy is natural. It actually takes hard work. It takes practice in recognizing our emotions, sensations, and thoughts to begin with. And it takes effort to manage our mind's critical comments and build buoyant beliefs.

There are times that our critical comments feel more real and authentic than buoyant ones. This is because we see the size of our trials and are intimidated by them. It is also because we are used to listening to critical comments.

Believe it or not, most people have an inner critic that is happy to point out their shortcomings. When we believe them, the critical comments rob us of our confidence and lower our resolve to face our problems. They feel more real because they are the thoughts that we have paid the most attention to.

Building buoyancy means that we have to do the heavy lifting of building better thoughts. With practice and exercise, buoyant beliefs get more comfortable to say. Over time, they can feel more natural and authentic. We need these to combat the critical comments if we are to have a chance at building lasting buoyancy.

On the following pages are exercises designed to identify our mind's critical comments and promote our buoyant beliefs. Give them a try. Do your best.

Critical Comments vs Buoyant Beliefs

This exercise is about building buoyant beliefs. Identify a critical comment that you often believe. Find a buoyant belief that you like. Quietly think the critical comment. Then say "No!" followed by your chosen buoyant belief.

	Critical Comments	Buoyant Beliefs
Bravery	I'm too scared	I am strong enough!
	It's too hard	I've got this!
	I'm going to fail	I am going to do this!
	I don't have what it takes	I do have what it takes!
Resilience	I give up	I can do it!
	I can't get up	I'll try again!
	I just can't go on	Just one more step!
	It's too hard to try again	Try again!
Endurance	I give up	I won't give up!
	It's too hard	It's not too hard!
	I can't take much more	I can keep going!
	I'm done	I'm not done yet!
Acceptance	I can't change it	It's OK!
	I can't take it	I can do this!
	It can't stay like this	I'm OK with this!
	This is the worst thing	This isn't so bad!
Tenacity	I can't keep going	I can do more!
	I'm too tired	One more step!
	I can't hold on	I can hold on!
	It's taking too long	Just a bit longer…
Hope	It's no use	This will be good!
	There's no point	This is going to work!
	It's more of the same	Tomorrow will be better
	Why try?	Why not do my best?
Excellence	This is terrible	This is a good start!
	It's not good enough	It's good enough for now
	I don't care	I want to do my best!
	I never get anything right	I do get things right!

Building Buoyant Beliefs

This exercise is about building buoyant beliefs. Select one of the following statements that you like the best. Memorize it. Breathe slowly in and slowly out. Close your eyes and say the statement to yourself for 10 breaths. Say it like you mean it.

I *can* do this!

I *am* strong enough!

I have *practiced this*!

Just a *little bit further*…

I've *got this*!

I *can* do this!

I *am* good enough.

I *am* capable.

I *will* hold on.

I *can* bounce back.

Just *one more step*.

I *can* do better!

I *will* learn from this!

I *am* courageous.

I *am* not listening to fear.

This *will* be alright.

Just relax and stay calm.

Just do your *best*!

It is *going* to be OK!

Doing The Work

Work hard, be kind, and amazing things will happen.

~Conan O'Brien~

True Story. I think I was age 6 or 7 at the time. Though my memories as I get older have tended to rust a bit, my memory about the event is as clear as the day it happened. It was most likely mid-week, and the day was sunny, warm, and it was the middle of summer. There were a few fluffy white clouds that hung overhead, and there was a gentle breeze that took the edge off of the heat. What made this day special was that I was going with my older sister and neighborhood friends to swim at the local outdoor pool.

I lived in a small town in the middle of Canada for much of my early childhood. And in our town, there was a modest size outdoor community pool. The summers were hot where I lived, and the pool was a raucous gathering place for most of the kids that loved being out of school for the months-long break. The water had been warmed by the summer heat. We could play at the pool all day long.

When I grew up, safety was an assumed privilege by most parents. They would simply pull up in their cars, deposit their kids at the community pool, and then drive away. The lifeguard would keep us safe for the day - or so they thought. All the parents had to do was arrive at the end of the day to collect their tired children.

Like many small kids, I loved the pool. There was always someone to play with, and fun was on the schedule all-day-long. On this particular day, I found myself holding on to the pool-ledge, inching my way closer to the deep end of the pool. This is where all of the big kids swam. It looked fun. Before long, I was well over my head in the deepest part of the pool. But since I was still holding on the ledge, I was still safe.

I am sure that it was a fleeting lapse in my impulsive child-like judgment or my hurried childhood non-awareness of my mortality, but at one moment, I thought I would just let go of the ledge and swim like all of the big kids. The only problem with the plan was that I didn't know how to swim. No one had ever taught me how. It didn't cross my mind that I couldn't do it. It looked easy.

There were so many thoughts that were going through my mind not long after letting go of the side of the pool. "Why was I sinking below the water?" "How do you breathe without inhaling water?", "Why aren't my flailing arms keeping me afloat?", "I thought swimming was supposed to be easy." My little mind raced as it searched for answers.

It was at the same time that I managed to get a hold of the side of the pool that the lifeguard showed up to help me. It couldn't have been more than a few seconds, but at the time, it felt as if time had stood still. My sister was too caught up in her own play to notice that I had gone toward the deep end. My friends were still in the shallow end playing, laughing, and having fun, oblivious to my plight. No one knew.

I never did tell my parents about it. My mom had a younger brother, Bill, who had drowned the year before I was born. She didn't talk about it much. It was too painful, I guess. He had never learned to swim. He jumped out of a canoe, assuming that the water was still shallow enough to touch the bottom of the lake. If I told her, my sister would get into trouble for letting me out of her sight, I would get a never-ending lecture on the rules of safety on the water, and I would have to be *supervised* at the pool for the rest of my summer. These options were just not acceptable.

You'd think that something traumatic like almost drowning would make me fearful of pools for the rest of my life. It didn't. As I grew older, I took swimming lessons. Instructors would show us how to breathe while doing the front crawl. They would coach us on how to hold our breath to 'drown-proof'. To my surprise, a person could stay buoyant through the way that they managed their breath. I also learned how to work the mechanics of my body to move through the water, under it, or to stay on top of it. With practice, I even got pretty good at it.

If I had been traumatized by nearly drowning, it might be a different story. I might feel fear whenever I came near a pool. I might have butterflies in my stomach or have stress headaches thinking about an upcoming swim event with my friends. I might even tell myself all kinds of reasons why I hate swimming, or why I could never learn. The truth is that at one point in my life, I didn't know how to swim, but with a little coaching, practice, and persistence, I learned just fine.

The same is true for buoyancy. Avoiding a trial doesn't make it go away. Facing it is the only way through it. With practice, it can get easier. You just have to START.

Think about the action of building something and breaking something for a moment. Both of them take energy and effort on our part. One builds up. The other tears down. The same is true for avoiding trials or facing them. Public speaking, singing out loud, going on a first date, solo-dancing - all of them can be absolutely terrifying to a person- until they learn. They just haven't done it, yet.

Knowing that you have to do it can provoke fear, weird sensations, and swirling thoughts. And it takes an incredible amount of energy to continue to avoid the trial if you can't get out of doing it. But it also takes energy and effort to face it head-on. Avoiding will always give the trial power over you. Facing it empowers and strengthens you with skills you never knew you had - yet.

Dr. Shelly Gable coined the term "active constructive responding". In her work, she developed a model of how to talk to others. If someone compliments your shirt, you have a choice of how to respond: actively or passively. You can also reply with responses that either construct (Build) or destroy (Break) relational goodwill.

An active, destructive response to the shirt-compliment could be a sarcastic "Sure. Thanks. What do you want?". A passive destructive response could be a self-mocking "What, this old thing?". A passive constructive response could be "I like your shirt too.". An active constructive response could be "Thank you so much for noticing. It's my favorite".

As Dr. Gable's model suggests, there are ways to build relationships and ways to break them. Both require a response. The same is true for building or breaking our own Bravery, Resilience, Endurance, Acceptance, Tenacity, Hope, and Excellence. Building buoyancy is dependent on taking steps (active and passive) that exercise and build its growth.

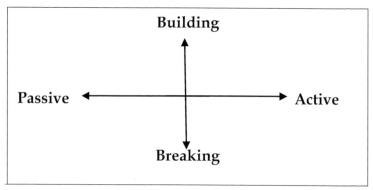

Now let's take a look at an example "trial." Most people (kids and adults) are afraid of public speaking. So let's imagine that a person has to give their first public speech to a large group of people. For effect, let's imagine that 200 people will be in the auditorium to listen. For most people, the emotion of fear, stressed bodily sensations, and critical thoughts will have been easily identified. Now what?

The answer depends on whether a person wants to face their fear and build their buoyancy, or avoid it and break their buoyancy. Let's assume that the person is too fearful and wants to avoid their trial. There are many ways to actively and passively break a person's buoyancy. They can ignore the date and time of their speech. They can feign illness. They can focus on the problem, or their feelings, or their lack of preparedness. They can blame others for their predicament or pick arguments. There are no shortages of strategies for how a person can avoid facing their trial. But in each case, the person ignores taking the responsibility to face their fear. And in doing so, they limit their own growth.

Now let's imagine that a person wants to face their trial. They may still have fearful emotions, stressed bodily sensations, and critical self-talk. But if a person realizes that part of their work is to take baby-steps: to try, to fall, to pick themselves up, and try again - then they are on their way to building buoyancy. Buoyancy needs exercise. Work it out, and it gets stronger. With strength, it can take on more challenges. This is the work.

If you look back throughout this book so far, you will notice something. Every time that I have introduced an exercise, I have encouraged you to "Give it a try" and to "Do your best." While building buoyancy, half of the work is in the "trying" something that builds buoyancy. It is in the TRYING that a person commits to movement. They risk failure. But they also promote growth. To paraphrase G.K. Chesterton, anything worth doing well is worth doing poorly at first. It all begins with *trying* to do it.

The other half of the work is to "Do your best" when you are trying it out. At any given time, if you do your best, you've done all that you can do to build the muscles of bravery, resilience, endurance, acceptance, tenacity, hope, and excellence. Doing your best is all you are responsible for, and accountable for.

Another thing that can help to promote buoyancy is to map out ideas and strategies that promote "building." This means thinking about (and possibly writing out) both active and passive building strategies to face the trial. So - back to the example of public speaking.

Active building strategies might be for the person to ask someone to coach them about public communication. Another might be to actively research their topic; or write the speech out, to practice it in front of a mirror, or to use a video recorder to see what they look and sound like. Another strategy could be to visit the auditorium that they will speak at or to visualize and imagine communicating in front of an audience. Even saying out loud to yourself Buoyancy statements is helpful. 'I can do this!', Just do your best.', and 'I *am* courageous.' Can all help a person to feel more confident in their task.

Passive building strategies could also be used to promote buoyancy in the face of the trial. Practicing calm breathing, grounding strategies, or rehearsing buoyancy belief statements would all passively help a person to lean into the calm before their storm. Thinking 'I've practiced this.', or 'Just breathe, and do your best' can go a long way in promoting confidence. Even, listening to calm music, having a relaxing spa-day, exercising, going for a run, doing yoga, and other activities can also promote an attitude that is more ready to face the challenge.

Passive Building	Active Building
Calm Breathing	Research the topic
Grounding strategies	Write the speech out
Rehearsing Buoyant Beliefs	Practice in front of mirror
Calming music	Video record
Day spa	Visit auditorium
Exercise (yoga, run, etc.)	Visualize communicating
Think, *'Just breathe!'*	Say out loud, *'I can do this!'*
Passive Breaking	**Active Breaking**
Ignore the speech	Call in sick instead
Play video-games	Get expelled
Think, *'I will look silly!'*	Say out loud, *'This is stupid.'*

At the beginning of the book, I noted that buoyancy employed the "attitudes and actions" related to bravery, resilience, endurance, acceptance, tenacity, hope, and excellence. The attitude most necessary in building buoyancy is the WILLINGNESS to face one's fear in the face of a trial. It is an attitude that does not shy away from the trial but instead remains steadfast in addressing it. It is the willingness to *try*, and the commitment to do your best. The actions most necessary for buoyancy are both passive and active in their orientation. They passively seek to minimize the stress applied to a person by the challenge. And they actively strategize and promote the strength and success of the person regarding their trial.

Proactively thinking about ways to use the Breaking & Building model can help a person strategize how to best face their challenges. It is through the exercise of the attitudes and actions related to buoyancy that a person will build it.

The next two pages are exercises for you to practice with. The first is a Building and Breaking practice sheet. It will help you to identify the ways that you can actively and passively build or break your buoyancy – or the ways you did so in the past.

The second exercise an example of how to think your way through a trial using the materials in this book. The example trial is 'speaking in public'. It shows how a person could identify their emotions, sensations and thoughts using the example above. It then helps a person to identify their critical comments and buoyant beliefs that they may use to encourage their forward progress. It then helps the person identify how they might be breaking their buoyancy and help them to strategize building it. It also asks a person to think about which element of buoyancy they need – bravery, resilience, endurance, acceptance, tenacity, hope or excellence. It is a good exercise in putting it all together, in order to do the work.

Building & Breaking Exercise

This exercise is about practicing using the Building & Breaking Model. Identify a trial that you had to face *in your past*. Use the model to identify what you did to actively build or break your buoyancy.

Variation: Think about a trial that you have to face in the future. Use the model to identify how you can build or break (actively or passively) your resilience in this challenge. (A full-page Building and Breaking sheet is at the end of the book).

Passive Building	Active Building
Passive Breaking	Active Breaking

Building Buoyancy: Speaking Example

What's the Trial?   Speaking in front of others.

What Emotions do I Feel?   Anxious, nervous, fearful.

What Sensations do I Feel? Tight muscles, stomach-butterflies.

What Thoughts am I Thinking?   'I can't do this.'

What are the Critical Comments I believe?
- 'I am going to look so silly.'
- 'I am going to fail.'

What are the Buoyancy Beliefs I can hold on to?
- 'I am smart.',
- 'I am entertaining'
- 'I can do this!'
- 'Everyone gets a bit nervous when they speak in public.'

What am I doing to Break my Buoyancy?
- Doing nothing/ Not preparing. Worrying.

What can I do to Build my Buoyancy?
- I can practice grounding, do a body-scan.
- I can write out my public talk. I can rehearse my talk.
- I can 'check out' the auditorium. I can imagine presenting.
- I can calmly breathe the 'Shhh' exercise. Listen to calm music.
- I think to myself 'I can do this!', 'Just breathe.'
- I can say out loud my favorite Buoyancy Belief.

What Do I Need?
Bravery: Press On
Resilience: Bounce Back
Endurance: Hold On
Acceptance: Letting It Be
Tenacity: Stick With It
Hope: Expect The Best
Excellence: Do My Best

A Final Word

I like the Conan O'Brien quote at the beginning of this chapter *'Work hard, be kind, and amazing things will happen'*. It really is true. The hard work begins with the attitude of *willingness* to try new things. It continues through the actions of awareness of our emotions, sensations, and thoughts. The hard work continues through learning to calm our breathing, learning to challenge our mind's critical comments with buoyant beliefs. It continues even further through the visioning and application of actively and passively building our buoyancy.

Whether we are talking about bravery, resilience, endurance, acceptance, tenacity, hope, or excellence - all require our hard work, our *best effort* to become stronger. No one else can do it for you. It was required of Joe Simon, Simon Yates, Kieran Behan, Earnest Shakleton, Alana Nichols, Dick and Rick Hoyt, Terry Fox, and Simona Atzori. It is required of you.

No one said it would be easy. Just as with the people mentioned, building buoyancy requires that you dig deep, do the work, and give it your all. Buoyancy requires it of you.

And in the effort of working hard, it is essential to "BE KIND" to others and yourself. The world has enough critical voices. It doesn't need one more. When you see someone struggling to learn something new - cheer them on. Say something kind, tell them that you are proud of them, or that they are doing *good work.*

And above all, be kind to yourself. When you try something, do your best. Expect to do it poorly at first - you WILL get better at it - with practice. And go easy on yourself. Risking learning something new means risking failure. Failure feels vulnerable and raw. You don't need to be the lone voice that criticizes your effort. Be kind to yourself. If you did your best today - great! If not - do better tomorrow.

Anything worth doing takes trying *and failing*, and trying again. Whether it is learning to walk, ride a bike, learning to speak in public, learning to swim, making new friends, doing a test - trying, and doing your best is all that is asked of you. The same is true for learning to be brave, resilient, enduring, accepting, tenacious, hopeful, or excellent. Do this, and amazing things *will* happen!

Building Buoyancy Exercise Sheet

What's the Trial?

What Emotions do I Feel?

What Sensations do I Feel?

What Thoughts (Critical Comments) am I Thinking?

What are the Buoyancy Beliefs I can hold on to?

What am I doing to Break my Buoyancy?

What can I do to Build my Buoyancy?

What Do I Need?
    Bravery: Press On
    Resilience: Bounce Back
    Endurance: Hold On
    Acceptance: Letting It Be
    Tenacity: Stick With It
    Hope: Expect The Best
    Excellence: Do My Best

Chapter Summaries: Key Concepts

When your heart speaks, take good notes.

~Judith Campbell~

Chapter 1   Buoyancy: What Is It?

Buoyancy is a word that relates to floating. It is what helps things to remain above the water line, and not sink. Psychological buoyancy relates to the characteristics and elements of human flourishing.

Where stress, challenges, and difficulties can make people feel down, buoyancy helps people to stay up. 7 characteristics related to human buoyancy are arranged in the acronym BREATHE. They are:

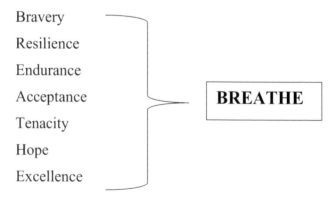

Bravery

Resilience

Endurance

Acceptance

Tenacity

Hope

Excellence

BREATHE

Chapter 2   Bravery: Pressing On

Bravery considers the attitude and actions related to *pressing on* despite trials, fear, challenges, or adversity. Fear is a common emotion when we face a trial. Fear can make us want to back down or run away from the challenge. Buoyancy requires that we face our fear with bravery and continue to press onward.

Chapter 3   Resilience: Bouncing Back

Resilience considers the attitude and actions related to *bouncing back* from trials, adversity, challenges, and setbacks. Sometimes, we get knocked down. Adversity will tell us to give up and remain stuck. Buoyancy encourages us to be resilient and to get back up and try again.

Chapter 4   Endurance: Holding On

Endurance considers the attitude and actions related to *holding on* despite trials, challenges, or difficult circumstances. Sometimes adversity causes us to believe that we can't take much more. Buoyancy encourages us to practice endurance, keep holding on and to persevere.

Chapter 5   Acceptance: Making Peace

Acceptance considers the attitude and actions related to *making peace* with trials, adversity, challenges, or difficult circumstances. Adversity will try to convince us that we can't deal with our circumstances. Buoyancy encourages us to practice acceptance - that things will be OK, that we can embrace the challenge, or integrate its lessons.

Chapter 6   Tenacity: Sticking With It

Tenacity considers the attitude and actions related to *sticking with it*, despite trials, challenges, adversity, or difficult circumstances. Adversity will try to convince us that the challenge is too hard, we are too tired, or it's taking too long. Tenacity will encourage us to go a little farther, or take just one more step toward success.

Chapter 7   Hope: Expecting the Best

Hope considers the attitude and actions related to *expecting the best* despite trials, adversity, challenges, or difficult circumstances. Adversity tries to convince us that there's no point. Hope encourages us that things will get better, and that there is a positive outcome just ahead.

Chapter 8   Excellence: Doing Your Best

Excellence considers the attitude and actions related to *doing your best* despite trials, adversity, challenges, or difficult circumstances. Adversity will try to convince us that we can't get it right. Excellence encourages us that we are off to a great start, and that we are getting better bit-by-bit. We just have to do our best. Our Buoyancy depends on it.

Chapter 9:   Building Buoyancy

Babies learn to walk through failure. They've never walked before, but they try it, and fail, and try again until they get it right. Many people don't like failure, so they avoid it. They don't realize that failure is a necessary part of learning.

Learning buoyancy means learning to pay attention. It requires learning to notice our emotions, sensations and thoughts connected to the trials we face. The TEST model helps people to identify what they notice.

When people are anxious, they breathe in a shallow fashion. When calm, they breathe in deeper and slower fashion. Practicing calm breathing helps to build buoyancy.

Chapter 10:   Putting It All Together

Trying not to think of flying pink unicorns just makes them appear. The same is true for our trials. The more we avoid them, the bigger they get. Our minds need a different target to make our trials more manageable.

Our minds are important in facing our trials. They can hold critical comments that weaken and break our buoyancy. Conversely, they can hold buoyancy beliefs that help build our buoyancy. What we focus on is up to us.

Chapter 11: Doing The Work

Building buoyancy requires work. It begins with noticing what we feel, sense and think – especially when we face life's challenges. The work continues in calming our bodies through the nature and quality of our breathing. Shallow and rapid breathing prolong our body's fear response. It also sustains our body's tension, limiting our ability to face the trial. Slow and deep breaths calm our bodies and help us to be buoyant.

In the same way, our thoughts can impair or promote buoyancy. Thinking critical comments can deflate our efforts or demoralize our will to try. Practicing buoyant beliefs can energize our resolve to remain engaged in facing life's challenges.

Building buoyancy also requires that we look at how we build or break it. Breaking buoyancy is either active or passive in avoiding our trials or sabotaging our efforts. Buoyancy requires that think of ways to passively build our will to face life's challenges. It also requires that we think of active ways to practice bravery, resilience, endurance, acceptance, tenacity, hope and excellence. Our buoyancy depends on it.

Further exercises and examples are provided to help you build buoyancy.

Give them a try.

Do your best.

TEST Exercise

This exercise is about identifying your Trial and noticing your Emotions, Sensations and Thoughts. Draw a face on the ginger-bread person's head. Think about a trial you are facing. Draw a circle around the emotions and sensations you feel. Write down your thoughts as well.

What's the Trial:_____

Thoughts

Basic Emotions
Anger
Surprise
Joy
Disgust
Sad
Fear
Love
Other?

Sensations
Butterflies in
Stomach
Heavy legs
Weak in the Knees
Nauseaus
Tingly Feelings
Light-headed
Clammy Hands
Temple Pressure
Shaky
Eyes Wide Open
Other?

What's the Trial:_____

Thoughts

Emotions

_____
_____
_____
_____
_____
_____
_____
_____
_____

Sensations

_____
_____
_____
_____
_____
_____
_____
_____
_____

Example Trial: Making New Friends

Building

Give a genuine smile	Say 'Good Morning' to them
Observe what they like	Compliment them
Be curious about them	Ask them about themself
Withhold criticism about them	Offer to help them
Leave them a treat	Ask them to join you
Be polite	Be kind
Use your manners	Say 'Thank-you'
Leave them a 'kindness card'	Celebrate with them
Think: 'I can do this.'	Say out loud: 'I am likable.'

Passive ◄——————————————► **Active**

Ignore them	Criticize them
Use silence	Take something without asking
Gossip about them	Call them a name
Be sarcastic	Lie to them
Don't keep your word	Mock them
Make faces at them	Yell at them
Be inflexible or rigid	Be clingy
Give in to them	Bicker with them
Think: 'They won't like me.'	Say out loud: 'I'm a loser.'

Breaking

Example Trial: Test-Anxiety

Building

Passive	Active
Practice calming breathing	Study
Listen to study music	Do a practice exam
Create a study space	Ask for help studying
Write study cards	Review study cards
Form a study group	Study with your group
Ask the teacher about the test	Talk about test ideas
Ask the teacher for old tests	Review old tests
Think: 'I can learn this.'	Say: 'I've got this!'
Ignore studying	Sleep in
Play video games	Skip school
Talk to your friends	Get expelled
Text people	Forget its test day
Eat ice cream	Leave the classroom
Watch Youtube	Sit and ignore the test
Daydream	Get caught cheating
Think: 'What's the point?'	Say: 'This is stupid.'

Breaking

Building Buoyancy

What's the Trial?

What Emotions do I Feel?

What Sensations do I Feel?

What Thoughts (Critical Comments) am I Thinking?

What are the Buoyancy Beliefs I can hold on to?

What am I doing to Break my Buoyancy?

What can I do to Build my Buoyancy?

Do I Need?
>   Bravery: Press On
>   Resilience: Bounce Back
>   Endurance: Hold On
>   Acceptance: Letting It Be
>   Tenacity: Stick With It
>   Hope: Expect The Best
>   Excellence: Do My Best

How Many Times This Week Have You Built Your Buoyancy?

	Mon	Tues	Wed	Thurs	Fri	Sat	Sun
Bravery							
Resilience							
Endurance							
Acceptance							
Tenacity							
Hope							
Excellence							

How Many Times This Week Have You Built Your Buoyancy?

	Mon	Tues	Wed	Thurs	Fri	Sat	Sun
Bravery							
Resilience							
Endurance							
Acceptance							
Tenacity							
Hope							
Excellence							

How Many Times This Week Have You Built Your Buoyancy?

	Mon	Tues	Wed	Thurs	Fri	Sat	Sun
Practicing Awareness							
Body Scan							
Grounding: Fingers							
Grounding: Toes							
Grounding: Breathing							
Breathing: Shh							
Breathing: Buoyant Beliefs							
Critical Comments/ Buoyant Beliefs							
Building Buoyant Beliefs							
Active & Passive Building							

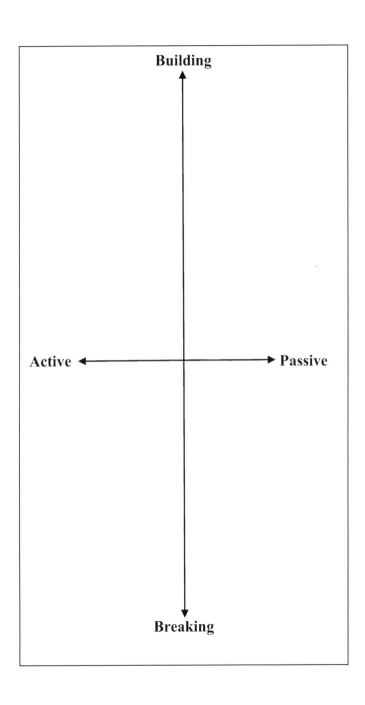

Notes:

Notes:

Manufactured by Amazon.ca
Bolton, ON

29190722R00087